Medical Ethics
in Imperial China

Paul U. Unschuld

Medical Ethics in Imperial China

A Study in Historical Anthropology

University of California Press
Berkeley • Los Angeles • London

University of California Press
Berkeley and Los Angeles, California

University of California Press, Ltd.
London, England

Copyright © 1979 by
The Regents of the University of California

ISBN 0-520-03543-7
Library of Congress Catalog Card Number: 77-80479
Printed in the United States of America

1   2   3   4   5   6   7   8   9

Contents

Preface and Acknowledgments   vii

1. Introduction   3

Medical Systems, Resources, Professionalization   3

Interests, Ideologies, Ethics   5

Formulated Ethics   11

Medical Resources, the Physicians' Code of
Ethics   12

2. A Conflict over the Distribution of
Medical Resources   15

Medical Practice and Experts in Ancient China   15

Annotated Texts on Ethics of Physicians and the
Confucian Reaction   24

*Sun Szu-miao and the origins of the debate on
medical ethics in China*   24

A Confucian response   35

Chu Hsi's stigmatization of medicine and some
    replies by practitioners   38

Confucian scholar physicians enter the debate   42

Doubts are voiced by scholars concerning the
    Confucian attitude towards medicine   53

The categorization of healers   58

Further statements from Confucian physicians   60

A shift in emphasis: Confucian and common
    physicians compete for patients   68

Orthodox Confucianism criticizes the degree of
    professionalization reached by practitioners   85

Further efforts to upgrade the moral value of
    professional healing   95

The end of the debate on ethics: persistence of
    social conflict and group heterogeneity   106

3. Concluding Remarks   115

Glossary   123

Bibliography   129

Index   133

Preface and
Acknowledgments

The problem of expertise is a social phenomenon ubiquitous in complex cultures. Expertise may provide power to a small group while alienating a majority of individuals from control over cultural activities in which they are heavily involved. In this study I demonstrate how the society of imperial China, dominated for the most time by Confucianism, responded to the problem of expertise in relation to healing. Although the traditional culture of China in general and many of its social institutions in particular have often been regarded as incomparable with corresponding Western phenomena, it will become obvious that the issues encountered are familiar to our own time and experience. Many of the arguments quoted here from former centuries appear relevant to current discussions; we may be reminded, for example, of the debate on being "red and/or expert" in contemporary China, or of bioethical debates in the United States.

The Chinese sources which I translated for this analysis were available for the most part in libraries in the United States. I wish to acknowledge here the generous support by the Harkness Foundation of the Commonwealth Fund of New York which enabled me to visit these libraries. I express my gratitude especially to Mr. James Shih-kang Tung, curator of the Gest Oriental Library, Princeton University, for his wholehearted assistance in my research, and to Dr. Wolfram Eberhard, professor of sociology,

viii *Preface and Acknowledgments*

University of California at Berkeley, who read the first draft of the original manuscript, for his many valuable comments.

This book is a revised and expanded version of the German edition, *Medizin und Ethik: Sozialkonflikte im China der Kaiserzeit,* published by F. Steiner Verlag, Wiesbaden, in 1975. Translation was made possible through a grant from the Wenner-Gren Foundation for Anthropological Research. Dr. M. Sullivan, Baltimore, rendered the original monograph into English. I am also very grateful to Dr. David V. McQueen and other colleagues in the Department of Behavioral Sciences, School of Hygiene and Public Health, The Johns Hopkins University, Baltimore, for their discussion and constructive criticism of the ideas presented here.

P. U. U.
Baltimore, March 1978

Medical Ethics
in Imperial China

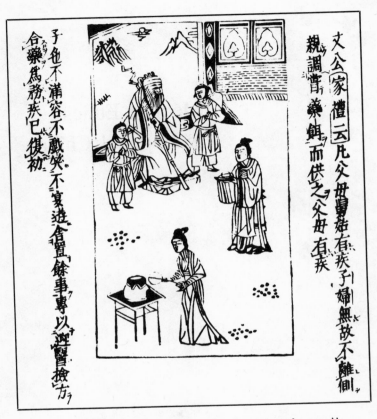

"Sons and their wives taste the drugs in advance."

An illustration from an edition of the *Hsiao-hsüeh*, compiled and commented upon by Chu Hsi (A.D. 1130–1200), published in 1658. The text in the marginal column reads as follows: "In the *Domestic Customs* by Wen-kung [i.e., Chu Hsi] it is stated: If the parents or the parents-in-law fall ill, the sons or their wives are not allowed to leave their side without reason. They have to prepare the drugs themselves, taste them in advance, and administer them [to the sick]. If the parents are sick, it is forbidden for their sons to display carefree conduct, to have fun or to look for pleasure. All other concerns have to be given secondary importance, so that they can devote themselves especially to their duty of receiving the physician, selecting formulas for prescriptions and preparing drugs. Once the disease has been cured, the original activities may be resumed" [Chu Hsi, *Hsiao-hsüeh chi-ch'eng,* Illustrations, p. 20b].

one

Introduction

Medical Systems, Resources, Professionalization

In order to compare the behavior of groups in relation to medicine, interculturally as well as intraculturally, I have employed several concepts. Before considering them as a basis for the arguments put forth in this study, it is appropriate to define the concepts in detail.

From the totality of its available resources every culture draws those which are necessary to satisfy health needs. Provided that it may be manipulated to bring about satisfaction, every material or non-material element within a culture may be a resource. Whether an element within a cultural domain becomes an available resource, meeting an individual's demand for satisfaction or serving a group to enforce its interests, depends on the relation of this element to the respective needs of individuals or groups.[1]

One cannot imagine that the control or possession of any one resource would guarantee satisfaction beyond a limited period of time. Hence it follows that every person depends on access to numerous resources to attain a lasting satisfaction. Some resources are abundant and can be utilized by every individual

1. Cf. Claude Lévi-Strauss, *The Raw and the Cooked.*

according to his needs; other resources are scarce and their distribution to a single person or to groups takes place on the basis of agreements; these agreements may be brought about peacefully or by force.[2]

We may say that the "medical system" of a culture is made up of a spectrum of resources that meet the demand for health care services, and the distribution pattern of possession and control over these resources. Here, as in other "resource categories," we distinguish between those resources which are abundant, such as oxygen in the air, and others which are extremely scarce, such as kidney dialysis machines. In the first instance there is no need for agreement concerning individual usage; in the second, agreements portending death for one and life for another must be made.

Each society develops a medical system differing in some respects from every other society's. The difference may ensue from the variety and particular nature of available resources; as, for example, when we compare the medical resources of the Navaho with those of a European country. Also, given equivalent types of available resources, it may manifest itself in different patterns of distribution, as, for instance, when we compare the medical systems of the U.S. and Sweden.

One can account in part for the growth of such diverse patterns through the ubiquitous process of "professionalization." "Professionalization" may be defined as the process by which one group (or number of them) endeavors to expand its possession of the medically related resources available in a culture, until it exercises exclusive control over those resources. In the field of medicine, "resources" may be differentiated as "primary" and "secondary." The "primary" resources are knowledge, drugs, skills, equipment and technology. The "secondary" resources are material and non-material rewards for medical services. This distinction between "primary" and "secondary" resources appears appropriate, in that generally access to the latter seems possible only through the former.

Medical professionalization as conceived here began in societies where the control and possession of the resources still remained in the family. At present, in industrial nations, medical professionalization has culminated in the concentration of re-

2. Cf. Paul E. White, "Resources as Determinants of Organizational Behavior."

sources in the hands of physicians, pharmacists, nurses and others, including various collectives such as the pharmaceutical industry and the hospital industry.

Professionalization includes nine dimensions: the acceptance of remuneration for services rendered; the use of technical terminology; the wearing of professional symbols; the passing of formal training; the emphasis on a professional ethics; monopoly and licensing; autonomy of the profession; internationalization; and social status. The relative development of these dimensions in a group indicates its degree of professionalization compared to other groups.[3] It is the intent of the present study to point out the role of ethics in the efforts of a group to reach a higher stage of professionalization.

Interests, Ideologies, Ethics

Professionalization is related to the changing distribution patterns of particular resources. In order to clarify the role of ethics in this process let us briefly consider the most important mechanisms effecting these changes.

One may assert that it is a universal phenomenon of persons or groups to strive for the possession of limited available resources. Further, this striving is often carried out at the cost of others. In primitive hunting and gathering communities the simplicity of the group and the idiosyncratic nature of the available resources prevent a member from making permanent any advantageous possession of resources. Nonetheless, even at this level of societal organization, in order to avoid conflict, overt and covert agreements are made to regulate the distribution of scarce resources.

In the traditional cultures based on agriculture and domestication we encounter an entirely different situation. Ever since the studies of Oscar Lewis,[4] we have known how profoundly life in these cultures is penetrated by suspicion and envy. His findings initiated a critical understanding which ended the "Arcadian myth" of innocence in rural societies, a myth which evidently extended as far back as Roman and Greek writings.

Suspicion and envy represent an efficacious manner of human

3. See Paul U. Unschuld, "Professionalisierung im Bereich der Medizin," and "Medico-cultural Conflicts in Asian Settings."
4. Oscar Lewis, *Life in a Mexican Village.*

conduct. In societies numerous symbolic gestures and rituals serve exclusively to prevent or diminish envy and suspicion. Envy as a theme is too far-reaching to consider at length in the framework of this discussion. I merely allude to it as an index of an almost universal awareness that others desire the advantage of possessing certain resources.[5]

In many cultures, whether large or small, simple or complex, mechanisms developed to stimulate a redistribution of any one-sided accumulation of resources. For example, the *kula* institution of the Trobriand Islands may be interpreted in this way; similar are the potlatch institutions of the Kwakiutl in British Columbia, of the Bakweri in West Africa, and of other nations. Similarly we can explain the enormous expenditures which are demanded from individuals in traditional societies on the occasion of the sumptuous fiestas in Latin America, if they are suspected of possessing more resources than their fellow-men. In our own society progressive taxes are ultimately founded on this very principle, either explicitly or not.

In addition to these rituals, various societies have followed certain concepts which link the causation of illness to inappropriate accumulation of scarce resources by individuals. Illness, in such instances, is presumed to have been sent as a form of punishment or sanction by ancestors,[6] or it may have been caused by some envious community member.[7] Where such concepts are accepted as truth, people who wish to remain free from illness are strongly discouraged from upsetting the equalitarian resource distribution pattern in their respective society.

How then, considering these and other protective and equalizing mechanisms, are individuals and groups able to alter the pattern of distribution of resources to their advantage? A factor which can yield quick results is certainly violence; restructuring by violence will not, however, be considered here.

A second mechanism is based on convincing a community or society that it will be to its advantage to concede control of certain resources to specific individuals or groups. Groups obtain this

---

5. Cf. Helmut Schoeck, *Der Neid und die Gesellschaft;* see also George Foster, "The Anatomy of Envy."
    6. See, for instance, Irving A. Hallowell, "Ojibwa world view and disease."
    7. See, for instance, June Nash, "The Logic of Behavior"; also Clarence Maloney, *The Evil Eye.*

control chiefly through the use of paradigms, i.e., models of explanation of a materialistic, religious or other nature, that justify or legitimize their control of resources. Based on recent evidence, I argue that such mechanisms are usually used deliberately, although this cannot be shown in every case. Man has always created a copious "pool of ideologies" or paradigms, from which individuals or groups are able to draw the paradigms closest to their interests.

We must concede that these ideologies are propounded not only for the purpose of "social change," as we tend nowadays to label the redistribution of available resources, whether by violent or peaceful means, but also for the purpose of reinforcement of existing patterns of distribution, be they the outcome of forceful upheaval or peaceful development. China in the latter Chou period and the beginning empire offers us an excellent example. From a "pool of ideologies" of several different paradigms that can still clearly be recognized (i.e., Confucianism, Taoism, Mohism, Legalism, to name the most influential ones), the state of Ch'in drew the most appropriate model for its progressive interests,[8] namely Legalism, and thereby brought the whole of China under its control. It was but a short time later, following the overthrow of the Ch'in, when the Han dynasty had been established, that the leading figures recognized Confucianism, which could be drawn from the same "pool," as an ideal paradigm which corresponded to their conservative interests,[9] and with it tried to maintain the existing pattern of distribution of the available resources. In doing this the powers in the Han dynasty exerted an influence which lasted for almost two thousand years.

The ideologies which I consider here are "comprehensive paradigms" (*Totalparadigmata*), that is, models of explanation which claim to include all the circumstances of existence. To these paradigms belong religions and various secular social theories, such as Confucianism and Marxism. Yet "partial paradigms" (*Partialparadigmata*) can be adopted too; these are models of explanation which do not claim to include all the circumstances of existence. An example of a partial paradigm is the

8. "Progressive" is defined here as characterizing the endeavor of a group to increase its share in certain resources available to a society.

9. "Conservative" is defined here as characterizing the endeavor of a group to maintain its established share in certain resources available to a society.

myth of the uniqueness of the divine mission of a social elite which justifies its control of resources. There is no sharp boundary between a comprehensive paradigm and a partial paradigm. Rather we are confronted with a continuum.

Although they appear similar, the terms "partial paradigm" and "comprehensive paradigm" introduced here should not be confused with the terminology used by Karl Mannheim (1893–1947), namely what he calls "particular ideology" (*partikulare Ideologie*) and "comprehensive ideology" (*totale Ideologie*). Mannheim's notion of a "particular ideology" refers to ideas and conceptualizations deliberately selected by a specific group; his notion of a "comprehensive ideology," however, refers to the entire structure of consciousness of a group.[10] Only a superficial relationship exists between the ideas to follow and Mannheim's explanations, which were written in the context of a sociology of knowledge.[11] My interest is in the background of the development, continuation, and, ultimately, the disappearance of ideologies.

The term "ideology" or "paradigm," as I use it, is distinct from Mannheim's conception of the "ideal world" (*Weltwollen*). The term "ideal world" entails the notion of a certain "unreality," since the "ideal world" of a group is a desired rather than an actually perceived world. Contrary to this, the term "paradigm" as I use it contains the notion of a "perspective on the world as it is" (*Weltsicht*); that is to say, primarily an explanation of worldly phenomena and the relations between them and the prescriptions for behavior commensurate with the paradigm.

As a point of departure, I should like to discuss the propagation of a paradigm. At any given time various models of explanation are formed on the basis of cultural stimulation, be they of a comprehensive paradigmatic or a partial paradigmatic nature. Those persons who establish these models of explanation constitute a group. Motivation to develop a paradigm forms a continuum which theoretically ranges from one extreme, "purely intellectual interest in the relationships between phenomena," to another extreme, "active concern for the interests of a specific group in society, or of an entire society as competing with other societies."

10. Karl Mannheim, *Ideologie und Utopie*, pp. 7–11.
11. Karl Mannheim, "Das Problem einer Soziologie des Wissens," in Kurt Lenk, ed., *Ideologie, Ideologiekritik und Wissenssoziologie*, pp. 197–200.

Now this first group may be joined by a second group which has learned of the paradigm and is willing to support it, inasmuch as it corresponds to its interests. It is not necessary that the first group look for the support of this particular second group or welcome it. Conceivably a one-sided and unwanted alliance can take place between the first and the second group. In any event, the second group acts rationally, as it considers the support commensurate with its pattern of interests.

Furthermore, we may distinguish a third group, consisting of persons who are convinced, or favorably affected, by the mode of explanation contained in the specific paradigm, and who rely on it and support it for this reason. In the case of a "successful" paradigm this group is likely to be most numerous, for every successful paradigm creates its own "masses." "Masses" as defined here do not constitute any particular social class.

Finally, it is necessary for us to distinguish a fourth group. Here one identifies persons following a paradigm not from their own volition but only under pressure, which may assume many forms, ranging from social pressure, which one cannot or does not want to avoid, to violence.

Four counter-groups correspond to the four groups of followers. The first counter-group contests the accuracy of the paradigm and stands, therefore, primarily in conflict with the group (or specific individual) that devised it. The second counter-group opposes the proponents of the paradigm because its own interests appear to be jeopardized. The third counter-group is already prejudiced by other convictions to such an extent that it cannot or will not open itself to a new paradigm. The fourth counter-group, in its turn, takes a stand against a given paradigm, not of its own account, but because of pressure from other groups to which it is related.

This grouping constitutes a theoretical point of departure for the dynamics of the social process. It appears profitable to inquire for what reasons and in what manner individuals and entire groups change their stand, a process which we can empirically observe in the past as well as in our present. The processes included in this model are marked by the fact that it is unlikely that any person holds a relationship to a single paradigm only. Almost every individual finds himself dependent on at least one comprehensive paradigm and several partial paradigms. In this sense he may be included in several of the groups described above. The variety of paradigms to which a single person is subjected can give rise to conflicts, and the question of how these conflicts are generated and resolved or repressed is a subject worthy of further investigation.

Before venturing into the subject of ethics, to which this study is devoted, mention should be made of the valuation of paradigms. The notion of "paradigm" which I use not only contains the generally accepted notion of "ideology," but goes beyond it. The paradigmatic structure always starts from a model of explanation in which all or some aspects of the existence of humanity are touched upon. Those responsible for the design of a specific paradigm may have been convinced of the truth of their formulation, or from the beginning they may have constructed it as a "lie" or a "deceit." Only a term which allows for both possibilities permits us to summarize the different models of explanation and ideologies in a value-free manner.

It is important to consider whether there are objective norms to evaluate competing models of explanation. Questions such as whether Christianity is, "objectively" speaking, better than Islam, or whether Confucianism is "objectively worse" than Marxism, or whether secular social theories are to be given "objective preference" over religions, illustrate the absurdity of assuming "truly" objective criteria which would lead to a "correct" answer. Every judgment in the realm of these comprehensive paradigms is linked to the subjective notion of values held by an individual or a group. That is, it is linked to given personal or social objectives.

Even in the case of the evaluation of partial paradigms, subjective notions of value play an important role. If we ask, for example, whether homeopathy is "better" than chemotherapeutics we are presenting a question which assumes notions of value. That is, even a person who feels obliged to take sides must realize that he has made a decision subjectively by calling upon notions which relate to his view of nature. Similar subjective notions of value apply to questions in the purely economic or political domain of partial paradigms.

The absence of objective norms for an evaluation of paradigms and the close correlation of "successful" paradigms with the interest of individuals or groups explain, in part, why some models of explanation lasted for long periods.

Formulated Ethics

Ethics represent a partial paradigm of a special nature. The definition of ethics given by Max Scheler appears particularly appropriate to the concerns of this work:

By the "ethics" of a time (in the broadest sense) we mean the judgmental and linguistic formulation both of values and relations of value-ranks which are self-given in emotional intentionality and of principles of assessment and norm-giving founded on values and their relations of rank. Through procedures of logical reduction we can show that such principles are the general propositions from which the content of individual acts of assessment and norm-giving can be logically derived.[12]

Within this definition of ethics Scheler distinguishes further between:

the ethics that is "applied and used" by moral subjects (and here we must distinguish the explicitly "recognized" from the tacitly "recognized," which can be very different, the former being always far more rigid and strict than the latter) and the groups of ethical principles that are discovered by logical procedures for which an "applied ethics" furnishes the material.[13]

Only the "explicitly recognized" variant of "applied ethics" interests us here and it corresponds to what I have labelled the fifth dimension of professionalization with an "emphasis on a professional ethics."

When related to medicine, one observes a partial paradigm in the "explicitly recognized" variant of "applied ethics," which seeks both to explain and justify the medical activity of the group propagating this particular paradigm. These ethics are usually derived from a comprehensive paradigm dominating a given culture, more or less reinterpreted.

The use of the partial paradigm "ethics" to secure for oneself access to certain resources is not found solely among medical practitioners. Recently it was reported that the formulation of a code of "ethics" was on the agenda of an international conference of sociologists and social workers. This group sensed a need to disclose its ethic and to emphasize it in order to reduce the risk involved, for example, in research on certain illegal activities of

---

12. Max Scheler, *Formalism in Ethics and Non-Formal Ethics of Values,* pp. 307–8.
    13. Ibid.

motorcycle gangs. In order to obtain control over resources, in this case the potential to study marginal criminal groups, it was necessary for the sociologists to convince both the law-abiding public and the motorcycle gangs, with the help of a partial paradigm, of their trustworthiness, and of the usefulness of such research activity for the society as a whole.

Medical Resources, the Physicians' Code of Ethics

Physicians' development of a formulated ethics can only be understood from the peculiar nature of the resources in question. "Primary" medical resources differ from many other resources at the disposal of a society. Under favorable conditions not only the practitioner but also the person to whom they have been applied can benefit from their use. In an unfavorable case the application of "primary" medical resources may have fatal consequences for both parties; at any rate, this is the information earlier cultures have handed down to us. What made the use of these resources an extremely risky enterprise was a widespread suspicion that death or injury of a patient might have been premeditated by the practitioner involved.

Beyond this, in cases of success the practice of medicine allowed practitioners to acquire non-material or material rewards, and in case of failure forced them to protect themselves. A necessity to protect oneself has remained an issue for all medical groups to the present day. (It applies to only a few other groups which have acquired the possession of certain non-medical resources.) Generally three major mechanisms of protection developed in the course of medical history.

On the level of sorcerers, shamans and magicians, the responsibility for the outcome of individual therapeutic actions has often been denied, and treatment results have been viewed as an outcome of the will of supernatural powers. In some cases responsibility rested on the guilt of the victim himself. Yet such protective mechanisms lost their impact in two great cultures: in ancient Greece during the intellectual revolution around the fourth century B.C., leading to a new world view, and at approximately the same time in China, when similar developments led to the medico-philosophical system of correspondence.

Prognosis gradually replaced the old protective mechanisms. Many medical historians interpret prognosis as a practitioner's attempt to procure a good name for himself by making impressive forecasts of the progress of an illness. Yet this interpretation seems to me to be secondary. I am more inclined to see prognosis as a protective device for separating the curable patients from the incurable ones. The *ayurveda* physician of India still acts according to this maxim even today when asked to distinguish the *sadhyas* from the *asadhyas*.[14] Prognosis allows the practitioner to accept profitable cases for himself and to reject unprofitable cases.

We know that some practitioners reached a stage of skill in prognosis which was admired by contemporaries. And yet this protective mechanism has considerable drawbacks. For one thing, it offers results which are imperfect; undesirable consequences of the treatment can come about if the practitioner is not exceedingly careful. For another, this precaution leaves the practitioner with a great part of potential "secondary" resources unused, namely all the rejected cases which could have provided rewards.

All these disadvantages have been overridden by a third protective mechanism, namely the formulated ethics of physicians. In the Occident we find these, for the first time, in the form of the oath of Hippocrates. The Chinese variant will be dealt with in the second part of our study.

The emphasis on professional ethics was initiated by individual practitioners. As brought out above in the quotation from Max Scheler, such "explicitly recognized ethics" may differ greatly from the "tacitly recognized" variant of "applied ethics." More than twenty centuries passed after the Hippocratic oath was written before a body of medical practitioners was organized in the West, making possible, by means of group pressure, the spread and general acceptance of a "formulated ethics."

As far as the progress of professionalization is concerned, the emphasis on professional ethics has decisive advantages over prognosis. In diverting the interest of the public from the outcome of medical activity to its process, it allows the practitioner access to practically all the secondary resources. Ultimately this is the essence of formulated ethics. Such ethics are designed to persuade

14. Shiv Sharma, "Ayurvedic Medicine in Practice," p. 446.

the public that whoever is in control and possession of medical resources uses them in a morally trustworthy manner. Further, any negative results would be viewed as acts of "God" or "nature," beyond man's control.

The mere affirmation of a code of ethics will not suffice to establish public trust. For one thing "formulated ethics" utilize the relevant values of the comprehensive paradigms found in the public, but at the same time contain very concrete regulations of behavior for the individual physician. These regulations of behavior, as for example the forbidding of advertising, hardly seem to relate to ethics. Yet, as will be demonstrated later, all these dimensions of ethics have their rational function.

two

A Conflict over
the Distribution of
Medical Resources

Medical Practice and Experts
in Ancient China

Earlier publications which discuss in some detail the topic
"physicians in ancient China" inevitably give an ambiguous impression. Often proverbs and textual passages are cited in which
the Chinese physician is given a rating equal to that of a good
minister, or is held high in esteem. Other passages, however, are
quoted from which one might conclude that Chinese physicians
numbered among the lowest servants in the state. Repeatedly it is
pointed out that there were several classes of physicians, ranging
from the *ju-i* ("Confucian medical scholar") to the *ling-i* ("itinerant doctors announcing their services publicly with a bell").
The explanation of the social structure from which those con-
tradictions and ranking resulted remains vague.

In whichever form it is carried out, medical practice is viewed
as a necessity for the survival of both the individual and the
society in which he lives. We know communities which highly
restrict medical practice or which reject it entirely because of the
different paradigms they follow. Yet in almost every culture we
find an active acknowledgment of the need for health care practice. In other words, the use of medical resources and their in-

crease can generally be accepted as legitimate. What poses a problem is the question "*who* uses and controls these resources?"

At the beginning of the Confucian era in China various groups participated in the use of all the available "primary" medical resources. We can assume that the spectrum of these resources ranged from empirical knowledge of the simplest type to magical and demonological practices to the sophisticated medical philosophy compiled slightly earlier in the *Huang-ti nei-ching*. According to historical reports there were physicians who based their arguments on theories involving the concepts of *yin-yang* and the Five Phases while applying acupuncture as their treatment method of choice. Others made no use of these concepts and techniques but resorted to pragmatic *materia medica* in their practices. Still other specialists are mentioned who relied exclusively on magic and demonology. Many resources with differing degrees of sophistication, though, remained in the hands of laymen or, rather, families.[1]

This distribution of control or possession of available "primary" resources among the general public and various competing groups of expert practitioners was paralleled by the distribution pattern of control over "secondary" resources. That is to say, the control over the rewards to be obtained from the patients (or the "not-yet-patients" in the case of prophylaxis) remained partially with the general public itself and partially in the hands of therapeutic groups.

With the acceptance of Confucianism as the ideology of the state, beginning with the last two centuries B.C., there arose a political problem in regard to medical practice. Certain leading figures in the early Han dynasty took Confucianism from the existing pool of ideologies as a comprehensive paradigm. Confucianism alone corresponded to their conservative interests, in that the social structure espoused by Confucianism rests on the ideal of a fixed pattern of distribution of certain resources. Many of the political decisions made in later centuries reveal the endeavors of the ruling group to retain certain resources under their control or to distribute them among the general public in such a fashion that their accumulation in the hands of certain groups of specialists would not lead to social change. This policy affected

1. Bridgman gives a description of the social aspects of medical practices in ancient China B.C.; R.G. Bridgman, "La médecine dans la Chine antique."

the salt merchants, the military, financiers, physicians, and many others. Individual groups repeatedly attempted to gain control over financial, military, salt, or medical resources. At some point the Confucian ruling group always discovered that its loss of the control and possession of these resources could bring about social changes. The frequently expressed disregard of military personnel, financial well-being, or medical practice constitutes an ideologic variant of this ongoing struggle for resources. The dissolving of armies in times of peace, the repeated acquisition of the salt monopoly by the state, and other measures represent practical politics as viewed here.

Max Weber noted the lack of specialization in imperial China and spoke of a "society of laymen." He must have been considering only the ideals of Confucianism, because in actuality considerable specialization existed. For example, Robert Hartwell has shown that between A.D. 756 and A.D. 1082 there existed a professional financial trade which exerted a decisive influence on the formulation and execution of economic policies.[2] It is significant that after times of weakness or neglect among Confucian leaders or after periods characterized by intensive professionalization, such as during the amassing of a highly professional army, processes of deprofessionalization would be introduced to strip the groups with power of their resources.

This Confucian policy resulted in a dilemma, primarily for two reasons. On the one hand, there persisted the necessity to use certain specialized resources, either occasionally, as in the case of military resources, or permanently, as in the case of primary medical resources. On the other hand, as time passed the resources available in China increased, so that ever greater demands were made on their overall control. To distribute all resources equally might well have been the theoretically ideal situation within Confucian society. In medicine, efforts in this direction were seen, for instance, in the publicizing of prescriptions on posters at crossroads. Such a procedure is documented for the eighth century.[3]

As we will illustrate later by examples, medical knowledge was always considered to be a necessary part of the general educa-

2. Robert M. Hartwell, "Financial Expertise, Examinations and the Formulation of Economic Policy in Northern Sung China," p. 209.
3. Joseph R. Needham, *Clerks and Craftsmen in China and the West,* p. 280.

tion of a Confucian. This is also an outcome of the effort toward an equal distribution of resources. The intention was to prevent any permanent specialization and the formation of groups which would bring about social change. The apprehensions underlying this policy were well founded. This can be seen from the example of one of the most serious disorders which rocked the Confucian social structure at the very beginning of the empire. Around the middle of the second century A.D. several religious movements were formed in China and the number of their followers increased rapidly. In a more or less independent action the comprehensive paradigm of Lao-tzu (604–? B.C.) was adopted as the basis of these movements, which were later called part of Taoism. The origin of these movements and the basis of their early economic strength was founded on the successful use of certain primary medical resources which were unorthodox from the Confucian point of view, but which led to control over extensive secondary resources. The initiators treated the sick by means of various ritual procedures and had the families of the cured patients pay with a certain amount of rice every year. In addition they trained disciples who helped spread these movements and eventually introduced them in numerous provinces. These activities, as a consequence, led to the formation of a theocratic state within China itself. Finally the well-known revolt of the Yellow Turbans occurred, whose suppression by the government required several years. Historians view these upheavals as the ultimate cause of the fall of the later Han dynasty (A.D. 25–220).[4] One may suspect that it was the opportunities of political abuse, at least of the heterodox primary medical resources by Taoists, which contributed decisively to the misgivings about any group pursuing a medical activity outside the Confucian comprehensive paradigm. The historical events presented here should likewise be regarded as justification of a policy against medical expertise adopted by the orthodox Confucians, more particularly when that expertise was paraded as a profession in order to gain access to material secondary resources.

Despite these political fluctuations the diversity and number of medical experts never decreased, even after the rise of Con-

4. Holmes Welch, *Taoism, the Parting of the Way;* Paul Michaud, "The Yellow Turbans"; Werner Eichhorn, "Bemerkungen zum Aufstand des Chang Chio und zum Staate des Chang Lu."

fucianism. The medical resources which the Confucians appropriated came from the domain of a science whose basic concepts were also expressed both in the Confucian philosophy of history and in their social theory. The medicine of the Confucians did not suffice to satisfy all the needs of the population. This is similar to the present-day situation in the Third World countries where Western medicine will probably never fully suppress the native systems of healing. While this fact led to therapists such as magicians, shamans, priests, and others continuing their practice of older forms of medicine, the Confucians also created, by various regulations of their own, a demand for practicing physicians beyond the needs of the family.

Apart from the institutions originating in the seventh century for training physicians at the imperial court, there existed regulations for medical care of the armies by so-called "military physicians" (*chün-i*) dating back to earliest times, with the records accessible to us from as early as the third century B.C.[5] Beginning with the later Han dynasty, so-called "medical craftsmen" (*i-kung*) were appointed to the administrations in the capital and the provinces.[6] However, the records from the Chinese sources relating to this give no evidence of the extent to which such regulations were carried out and what functions these "physicians" had.

The initiative for lasting welfare regulations in civil life came from the Buddhists. The first description of a permanent hospital dates back to the fifth century A.D. It had been founded by a Buddhist prince in the state of the Southern Ch'i. Only two decades later the first public institution of a similar nature was established.[7] The subsequent developments afford an explicit example of the competitive efforts for new resources available to a society.

The idea of permanent hospitals should be considered as a primary medical resource introduced into China by the Buddhists, proponents of a comprehensive paradigm in competition with Confucianism. Apparently the Confucians discovered very soon that the control over this resource put an undesirable measure of social influence into the hands of the Buddhists, and with it power. Perhaps it was this reason which led so soon to the establishment of secular public institutions, which I view as a

5. Needham, *Clerks and Craftsmen*, p. 276.
6. Ibid., p. 381.
7. Ibid., p. 277.

phenomenon of the rivalry over "primary" medical resources leading to "secondary" resources. In my opinion the establishment of secular public hospitals cannot solely be based on a Confucian concern for the well-being of the people. This becomes even more apparent in later competitive struggles of the Confucians and Buddhists for resources. This struggle was carried out on many levels and in many areas besides the field of medicine. In A.D. 653 Buddhist and Taoist monks and nuns were excluded from medical activities.[8] In making the use of "primary" medical resources by Buddhists illegal, the Confucian interest groups obstructed access to "secondary" resources, the ultimate aim of any such restrictions. In A.D. 845, during the dissolution of monasteries, the Buddhist hospitals were given over to the control of laymen.[9]

Since these resources had already been introduced into Chinese society and their use in itself corresponded to Confucian values, such as "humaneness" (*jen*) and "compassion" (*tz'u*), they could not simply be neglected, let alone be abolished. Thus, during the centuries to come and in almost all the later dynasties, we may observe more or less extensive legislation for social services, with medical care for people, officials, soldiers, and inmates of prisons.[10] The appropriate establishments were staffed in part by officials who had to undergo medical training and thereafter take the pertinent examinations.

In the first half of the seventh century A.D. an imperial school of medicine was founded in the capital, and at the same time medical institutions developed in the most important cities of the

8. Ibid., p. 278.
9. Ibid.
10. For the temporary establishment of pharmacies on the basis of a welfare policy from the eleventh up to the fourteenth century, see Paul U. Unschuld, *Die Praxis des traditionellen chinesischen Heilsystems*, pp. 9–14; in addition to the source material cited there, we know today that such establishments were continued at least through the sixteenth century, and possibly up to the eighteenth century. Cf. Ch'iu Han-p'ing, ed., *Li-tai hsing-fa chih*, p. 595; and Chu Lun, *Hui-min chü pen-ts'ao shih-chien*, pp. 2b–4b. With the latter text cf. also Paul U. Unschuld, *Pen-ts'ao*, p. 213. For the time of the rule of the Mongols [Yüan dynasty, A.D. 1234–1367] numerous detailed instructions for the medical care of prisoners can be found in Shen Chia-pen, *Yüan tien-chang*, ch. 40, pp. 13b–16b, 21b–22a. The physicians to be drawn upon for the care of the prisoners are referred to here as *i-kung* ("medical workers"). *I-kung* was the designation for the lowest category of the officially employed physicians; the rank of civil servant did not befit them.

provinces. In line with the general policy of the administration, great efforts were made to incorporate medical training as a supplement to basic Confucian education. Needham writes that there was a marked effort in the Chinese Middle Ages to "raise the intellectual level of the physicians."[11] I conclude that the Confucian officials as a group wished to secure their control over "primary" medical resources, with the ideal of preventing the loss of their control over "secondary" medical resources. It is difficult to say how far they succeeded in doing this. Throughout the centuries there were famous physicians who worked at every level of society, up to the imperial court, without having emerged from an administrative career. Repeatedly we find remarks to the effect that renowned physicians, who had carried out a successful treatment at the court, were appointed to be civil servants as a mark of their distinction. In this manner outstanding physicians from the people were co-opted and artificially alienated from their original group, whose status they would otherwise have considerably advanced after such a success.

In addition to the politically motivated competitive struggle between the Confucians, the Buddhists, and the Taoists over medical resources,[12] a dispute arose between the Confucian medical officials and the "independently practicing" physicians. The borderline between these two groups was not always clear, because some Confucians failed to consider the saying of Confucius that "the scholar is not an instrument," and therefore carried out their medical practice as a livelihood. In this conflict both parties made use of a partial paradigm, which we would nowadays call "medical ethics" in the sense defined at the beginning of this study.

When the independently practicing physicians began their efforts to achieve professionalization, they constituted a group of non-related practitioners. This group was regarded with suspicion and contempt by the public. In his biography of the legendary physician Pien Ch'io, Szu-ma Ch'ien (145–80? B.C.) had the

---

11. Needham, *Clerks and Craftsmen,* p. 265.

12. Besides the groups mentioned, others were involved in the health-care system of imperial China. For the work of Muslim physicians at the time of the Mongols, cf. T'ao Tsung-i, *Cho-keng lu,* ch. 22, p. 14a; for the activity of Nestorian oculists and the destruction of the Nestorian colony in Szechuan in the late T'ang period (A.D. 618–907), cf. Li Te-yü, *Hui-ch'ang i-p'in chi,* ch. 12, quoted in Liu Ming-shu, "An Invasion by Nan Chao and the Destruction of the Nestorians at Chengtu," p. 30.

prince of Huan say to his court: "Physicians look out for profit, therefore they try to be of use to those who are not sick!"

In the first place the freely practicing physicians were opposed by Confucianism because of its inherent rejection of any extensive specialization, and then by the official physicians, who from the seventh century on had a formal education in addition to their training in classical studies. Up to at least the time of the T'ang (A.D. 618–906) their degree of professionalization was little higher than that of independently practicing physicians. A report from the dynastic history of the T'ang indicates clearly that these practitioners were still rated according to the success of their activity,[13] rather than according to the content and the care with which they carried it out; and this is already evident from similar reports in the *Chou-li* almost one thousand years earlier. The status of the craftsman who is judged according to his products had not yet been overcome.

A new development appears in the twelfth century A.D. Henceforth, in Hangchou, the candidates for the career of medical officer were to undergo comprehensive examinations in classical non-medical literature and philosophy on the one hand, and in medicine on the other hand.[14] To what extent these and other regulations of the qualifying medical examinations came into being administratively can be determined today only with great difficulty; documents which could give some information on the subject are extremely rare, so that we are in danger of inferring an assumed reality from the political intentions of certain groups. Among the few sources which give a different impression is a document from the year 1314, which was included in the collection of exemplary decisions from the Yüan period (A.D. 1234–1367, the rule of the Mongols) and which distinguishes itself by its singular colloquial style. In this piece of writing the author

13. Bridgman, "La médecine dans la Chine antique," pp. 192, 196; *Hsin T'ang-shu*, PNP, ch. 38, p. 16141; Needham, *Clerks and Craftsmen*, p. 387; the translation of the particular passage in the *Chou-li*, ch. 2, p. 1a, by E. Biot may give the misleading impression that the process of medical treatments carried out by civil servants was formerly evaluated. Biot spoke of "mistakes in the treatment" which constituted the basis of the evaluation. Yet as a matter of fact the specific term *shih* has to be understood in this case as "failure of the treatment," in opposition to *ch'üan*, i.e., "success in the treatment," "cure." Compare Edouard Biot, *Le Tcheou-li*, ch. 5, p. 93.

14. Needham, *Clerks and Craftsmen*, p. 391.

complains about the state of training of the highest medical officers practicing at the court, who were also sent away as professors to teach in the provinces. He points out the failure to adhere to the rules of the examinations and the widely spread nepotism contributing to the fact that numerous persons had obtained these specific positions without the necessary knowledge.[15] Since the Chinese dynasties were subject to the known cycle of rise and fall, we have to assume that the administrative regulations for the medical system also experienced their cycles of intensified and neglected execution.

In the abovementioned regulations from the twelfth century calling for comprehensive examinations we observe the influence of a Confucianism reinforced by Neo-Confucianism. From this point on there was an increased emphasis on the *ju-i* ("Confucian medical scholars") as distinct from the *yung-i* ("common physicians"). This manifests an effective attempt on the part of the Confucians to establish their control over medical resources. Compared to their independently practicing colleagues, the Confucian medical doctors possessed the full support of the Confucian comprehensive paradigm.[16] At least in theory their knowledge was, first of all, destined for the private needs of the family, and only then for a certain number of clients.

Therefore a group which was concerned with professionalization as such, but was opposed to this Confucian society and its medical doctors, had to endeavor, first of all, to reduce the suspicion (called forth by its opponents) in which it was held by the population. Secondly it was necessary for the group in question to adopt the values of the ruling group and to posit them as the basis for its activity, in order to have it authorized. To this a crucial third element can be added: the group had to strive continuously to increase and to perfect its "primary" resources in order to avoid the burden of failures. In this necessity a decisive impetus for medical progress may be seen. These three aspects of professionalization may be viewed as "tactical elements."

15. *T'ung-chih t'iao-ko,* ch. 21, pp. 5a–6a.

16. Relevant aspects of Chinese legislation during the Confucian epoch reflect these social processes. For an analysis of the history of malpractice legislation and jurisdiction in imperial China see Paul U. Unschuld, "Arzneimittelmissbrauch und heterodoxe Heiltätigkeit im China der Kaiserzeit."

Furthermore, regardless of the type of their practice, it was in the interest of all the physicians, be they Confucian or independent practitioners, to divert the attention of the public from the outcome of their activity to the process of their practice. Only a few individuals were sufficiently aware of both this interest and the three "tactical elements" of professionalization to reflect these phenomena in their writings. In the East as in the West, these people represented the pioneers of the professionalization of the entire group to which they belonged. One of the levels on which they were working to advance their interests is discussed in the following texts. This level partly manifests itself in ethics.

Annotated Texts on Ethics of Physicians and the Confucian Reaction

Sun Szu-miao and the Origins of the Debate on Medical Ethics in China

With the exception of several short quotations from earlier times the texts to be discussed in this study date from the seventh century A.D. up to the end of the nineteenth century. Following the explanations given above, one might assume that the debate over ethics in Chinese medicine coincided with the broadly conceived program for the training of medical doctors in the Chinese Middle Ages. Such an assumption would be quite risky; its sole justification may be the fact that we have no knowledge of an earlier Chinese source going beyond mere suggestions of ethics or discussing the ethics of the physicians at length.

The sources used here are taken from medical literature, with the exception of texts used for the explanation of some arguments. In part we are dealing with individual sections from medical literature which were devoted to questions of medical ethics. Although some of these statements are repetitive, I have translated every section on ethics which I could locate. I present them unabridged, in order to make this primary source material accessible to the widest possible audience. The goal is to create a basis for further discussion centering on the theme of ethics in medicine. In addition to these individual sections I have examined a considerable number of prefaces to medical literature for their relevant statements. In these cases I have had to make a selection from this prolific material. It is important to emphasize that the authors cited below took a definite stand in favor of medicine, either by editing medical literature itself or simply by composing prefaces to it. Thus they represent an aggregate who wish to influence the pattern of resource distribution to their private advantage or in the direction of the interest of the social group with whom they share a comprehensive paradigm. There are no "impartially objective" statements. Every participant may be identified with the interests of one of the groups involved.

The texts speak mostly for themselves. Wherever material was available, it seemed appropriate to provide the social background of the specific authors and to point out the central features of their formulated ethics.

Sun Szu-miao (A.D. 581?–682) appears to be the first Chinese author to have devoted a separate section of a paradigmatic nature to questions of medical ethics. In the official history of the T'ang dynasty[17] his biography describes him as an extraordinarily talented man, who devoted himself to the teachings of the *I-ching*, of Lao-tzu and of the *yin-yang* philosophers, and also took an interest in the magical calculation of numbers. Besides other smaller works, he compiled the lengthy *Pei-chi ch'ien-chin yao-fang* (generally known as *Ch'ien-chin fang*) and, three decades later, a supplementary work, the *Ch'ien-chin i-fang*. Both works have been often reprinted and still constitute an important source for the practices of traditional Chinese physicians.

Where or how Sun Szu-miao received his medical training is not known to us. It is, however, highly unlikely that he was in contact with one of the medical schools established after A.D. 629. Usually referred to as a Taoist, he seems to have been equally influenced by a considerable amount of Buddhist thought. He already possessed a strong reputation during his lifetime, based on his education and his achievements as a physician. This resulted in several appointments to positions at the court, none of which he ever accepted.

At the beginning of his voluminous work *Ch'ien-chin fang*,

17. An analysis of the available biographies of Sun Szu-miao can be found in Nathan Sivin, *Chinese Alchemy*, pp. 81–144.

Sun Szu-miao devoted a separate section "to the absolute sincerity of Great Physicians" (*"Lun ta-i ching-ch'eng"*).[18] It is important to call attention to several points which he touches upon in this section. In the first place, he gives a general frame of reference to "his" medicine. He does not provide many details concerning the concepts he thought a "Great Physician" should follow. Yet from the few terms he mentions it appears that he advocated the medicine of systematic correspondence only. This medicine was a syncretic conceptual system based on the theories of the Five Phases (*wu-hsing*) and *yin-yang,* as well as on a mode of treatment derived from the concepts of magical correspondence. Furthermore, its contents and its terminology were influenced by the concepts of demonic medicine. Sun Szu-miao could have chosen pure demonic medicine (of which he was a strong supporter elsewhere, as can be seen from his introductory remarks to his Classic of Spells [*Chin-ching*]) or he could have chosen pragmatic, symptom-oriented pharmacotherapy, or even the abovementioned "religious" medicine of some Taoist sects, as a theoretical basis for his and his colleagues' healing practice. This is especially so because demonic medicine and pragmatic pharmacotherapy may have constituted the most prevalent paradigms of medical practice among the populace of his time (and throughout all subsequent centuries until the end of the Confucian era). We do not know the reasons for Sun Szu-miao's decision to point out only the medicine of systematic correspondence as the basis of a Great Physician's practice. It should be mentioned again, though, that this system's underlying paradigm reflected the social concepts inherent in Confucian ideology. In contrast, demonic medicine and symptom-oriented, pragmatic pharmacotherapy flatly contradicted several claims and assumptions of Confucianism. Demonic medicine is based on a world view of "all against all," where one's own morality is neither an assur-

18. Tameto Okanishi, *Sung i-ch'ien i-chi k'ao,* p. 802 (table of contents of the Sung editions of the *Ch'ien-chin fang*). In an edition of the *Ch'ien-chin fang* from 1603, the same section is entitled "Lun t'ai-i ching-ch'eng" (cf. Li T'ao, "Chung-kuo ti i-hsüeh tao-te kuan," pp. 679–80). The term *t'ai-i,* which had been used since the earlier han period to designate the highest medical officials of the court, can be considered either as a misinterpretation of the group to whom Sun Szu-miao had devoted his section or as a simple typographical error. In the edition of the *Ch'ien-chin fang* by Chang Lu (1627–1707) the term *ta-i* can be found again; Chang Lu, *Ch'ien-chin fang yen-i,* ch. 1, pp. 1b–4a.

ance of a healthy life as an individual nor a guarantee of a harmonious existence in society. Pragmatic pharmacotherapy is equally amoral, in that it rests on an assumption that illness can be prevented or cured by the intake of certain substances and that, therefore, no specific moral lifestyle is necessary for maintaining or regaining health. Confucianism, however, closely ties together maintenance of social order and of individual health; its social ideology starts from the notion that a certain lifestyle along fixed moral rules will contribute to both social harmony and personal well-being. To be sure, the medicine of systematic correspondence as it has come down to us in its earliest texts, compiled between the second century B.C. and the eighth century A.D. (most notably the Yellow Emperor's Inner Classic [*Huang-ti nei-ching*]), also contains various allusions to Taoist concepts. Yet these are marginal and do not overshadow the basic parallels that exist between this healing system and Confucian ideas of a desirable social structure.[19]

Next to presenting "his" theoretical framework, Sun Szu-miao pointed out the necessity of a thorough education and rigorous conscientiousness. He may have done so in reference to the establishment of the first medical schools for Confucian scholar physicians during his lifetime, an innovation which may have been regarded by freely practicing physicians as jeopardizing their image.

Then follow explanations both on the basis of values, such as "compassion" (*tz'u*) and "humanity" (*jen*), and on the basis of maxims, such as "to aid every life and every man" or "one cannot destroy life, in order to save life," which are taken from the Confucian and Buddhist comprehensive paradigms.

Sun Szu-miao seems to have understood that when visiting the sick the psychological aspects of the relationship between physician and patient must be taken into account. In order to gain trust, and thus unhindered access to "secondary" resources of medicine (that is, material and non-material rewards), the physician has to appear affectively neutral. The first signs of a group consciousness appear in Sun Szu-miao's explanations, when he criticizes the habit of belittling other physicians for the sake of one's own advantage. This shortsighted conduct is a decided disadvantage

19. For an account of the different conceptual systems prevalent in the history of Chinese medicine see Paul U. Unschuld, "China."

for a group in the process of obtaining professionalization and yet, according to all reports, it was displayed by the majority of practitioners at that time and later. In our own past, outstanding leaders of various professions have noticed this tendency; they therefore organized smaller elite groups within their larger group of professionals. These select groups were open only to candidates who had given evidence of high quality of service. At the same time these core groups gave the impression of unity to the outside and avoided any critique of one another in front of non-members of the group. This was done in order to gain a much higher potential of trust and to obtain those resources which were not accessible to persons merely interested in individual profit.

The demarcation of a core group against the less exemplary mass is articulated in Sun Szu-miao by his choice of the term *ta-i* (closely related to *t'ai-i,* "court physicians") and his reference to the inefficiency of all the other physicians. For this reason he was not concerned with all the physicians, but only with those who stood out as "Great Physicians." To organize this elite group would have been a logical step, and in the West it was carried out, though considerably later. Yet in the Confucian society this did not happen.

In the end Sun Szu-miao deals with the problem of rewards. Greed was evidently one of the most serious grounds for the suspicion in which the public held the practices of physicians. Prince Huan of Ch'i made statements to this effect. If the public is to be persuaded that at least the "Great Physician" is not out for the material goods of his patients, one has to point out another system of reward, and make it sound credible that this compensates for the renunciation of the goods of those patients whom one wants to treat.

Sun Szu-miao referred back to a statement by the founder of Taoism, Lao-tzu (604–? B.C.), in order to depict an incentive for rewards which was to render material desires unnecessary. In claiming that good deeds would be rendered by one's fellow-men while bad deeds would be requited by spirits, he was not far from an emphasis contained in the Confucian comprehensive paradigm, namely the stress on a this-worldly "reward" by fame which will be retained in later generations. Also he came close to the Buddhist idea which respectively foresees reward or retribution by supernatural powers in either the present life or a later life, if not even in another world.

To sum up we can say that the explanations formulated in this manner were based on values and concepts immanent in the three comprehensive paradigms influencing Chinese society during the time of Sun Szu-miao with almost similar strength. In addition they were oriented toward the gain of trust and provided a protective function. This protective function is the essential trait of a formulated ethics. In order to draw a profile of himself and his "better" colleagues, Sun Szu-miao could, at least theoretically, have put the excellence of his product in the foreground. Yet for a brilliant thinker of the stature of a Sun Szu-miao, what was at stake was the transformation of the outcome evaluation of his activity into a process evaluation, in order to surmount the status of a craftsman. Here are his own words:

☐ *ON THE ABSOLUTE SINCERITY*
  OF GREAT PHYSICIANS

The saying goes back to Chang Chan [fourth century]: The difficult parts and the fine points in the [medical] classics and the literature on the prescriptions date back to the distant past.

Nowadays we have diseases which take a similar course with [different patients], yet from the outside they appear to be different; and there are others, which take a different course with [different persons], yet from the outside they appear to be similar. For this reason it will never suffice to examine exclusively with ears and eyes the symptoms of excess [*shih*] or deficiency [*hsü*] in the five granaries [*wu-tsang*] and the six palaces [*liu-fu*] as well as the flow [*t'ung*] or the blocking [*sai*] of the blood [*hsüeh*] and the pulses [*mai*], and the constructive [*jung*] and protective [*wei*] influences. In the first place one has to examine the symptoms of an illness which can be felt in the pulses to determine the specific ailment. Only someone who gives his undivided mental attention can begin to elaborate on these symptoms. This undivided attention must be given even to the last details which are related to the irregularities in the depth and the marking of the various kinds of pulsations [*ts'un, k'ou, kuan, ch'ih*], which condition the variations in the position of the acupuncture points [*shu-hsüeh*], and which are responsible for the deviations in the thickness and strength of flesh and bones. Today, however, the prevailing effort is to ,grasp the most subtle details with the crudest and most superficial thought. This is truly dangerous!

If there is an excess and we still increase it, if there exists a deficiency and even more is taken away, if a congestion prevails and is further intensified, if there is a flow and still more is drained, if there is chill and further cooling is applied, and if in the case of heat an increase of temperature is brought about, then the specific illness has to deteriorate exceedingly. Where there is still hope for life I then see the approach of death!

It has indeed never happened that spirits distributed [the understanding] for the difficult aspects and the details which are necessary for physicians, people versed in the prescriptions, soothsayers and magicians. But how else can a person gain access to these secrets? At all times fools could be found who studied the prescriptions for three years and then they simply maintained that there was no disease in the world which could not be cured. Thereafter they treated diseases for three years and reached the conclusion that there was no useful prescription in the world. Thence ensues that it is absolutely necessary for the student to master the foundations of medicine in its most general significance, and to work energetically and unceasingly. He is not to gossip, but has to devote his words exclusively to the medical teachings. Only then will he avoid errors.

Whenever a Great Physician [*ta-i*] treats diseases, he has to be mentally calm and his disposition firm. He should not give way to wishes and desires, but has to develop first of all a marked attitude of compassion. He should commit himself firmly to the willingness to take the effort to save every living creature.

If someone seeks help because of illness or on the ground of another difficulty, [a Great Physician] should not pay attention to status, wealth or age, neither should he question whether the particular person is attractive or unattractive, whether he is an enemy or a friend, whether he is Chinese or a foreigner, or finally, whether he is uneducated or educated. He should meet everyone on equal ground; he should always act as if he were thinking of himself. He should not desire anything and should ignore all consequences; he is not to ponder over his own fortune or misfortune and thus preserve life and have compassion for it. He should look upon those who have come to grief as if he himself had been struck, and he should sympathize with them deep in his mind. Neither dangerous mountain passes nor the time of day, neither weather conditions nor hunger, thirst nor fatigue should keep him from helping whole-heartedly. Whoever acts in this manner is a

Great Physician for the living. Whoever acts contrary to these demands is a great thief for those who still have their spirits!

From early times famous persons frequently used certain living creatures for the treatment of diseases, in order to thus help others in situations of need. To be sure, it is said: "Little esteem for the beast and high esteem for man," but when love of life is concerned, man and animal are equal. If one's cattle are mistreated, no use can be expected from it; object and sentiments suffer equally. How much more applicable is this to man!

Whoever destroys life in order to save life places life at an even greater distance. This is my good reason for the fact that I do not suggest the use of any living creature as medicament in the present collection of prescriptions. This does not concern the gadflies and the leeches. They have already perished when they reach the market, and it is therefore permissible to use them. As to the hen's eggs, we have to say the following. Before their content has been hatched out, they can be used in very urgent cases. Otherwise one should not burden oneself with this. To avoid their use is a sign of great wisdom, but this will never be attained.

Whoever suffers from abominable things, such as ulcers or diarrhea, will be looked upon with contempt by people. Yet even in such cases, this is my view, an attitude of compassion, of sympathy and of care should develop; by no means should there arise an attitude of rejection [in regard to the afflicted person].

Therefore a Great Physician should possess a clear mind, in order to look at himself; he should make a dignified appearance, neither luminous nor somber. It is his duty to reduce diseases and to diagnose sufferings and for this purpose to examine carefully the external indications and the symptoms appearing in the pulse [of patients]. He has to include thereby all the details and should not overlook anything. In the decision over the subsequent treatment with acupuncture or with medicaments nothing should occur that is contrary to regulations. The saying goes: "In case of a disease one has to help quickly," yet it is nevertheless indispensable to acquaint oneself fully with the particular situation so that there remain no doubts. It is important that the examination be carried out with perseverance. Wherever someone's life is at stake, one should neither act hastily, nor rely on one's own superiority and ability, and least of all keep one's own reputation in mind. This would not correspond to the demands of humaneness!

And then in visiting the sick, wherever beautiful silks and fabrics fill the eye, the physician is not allowed to look out for them either to the left or to the right. Where the sounds of string instruments and instruments of bamboo fill the ear, he should not evoke the impression that he delights in them. Where delicious food is offered in stunning succession, he is to eat as if he experienced no taste. And, finally, where liquors are placed one next to the other, he will look at them as if they did not exist. Such manners have their origin in the assumption that if one single guest is not contented, the whole party cannot be merry. A patient's aches and pains release one from this obligation less than ever! However, if a physician is tranquil and engrossed in merry thoughts, in addition to being conceited and complacent, this is shameful for any human frame of mind. Such conduct is not suitable to man and conceals the true meaning of medicine.

According to the regulations of medicine it is not permissible to be talkative and make provocative speeches, to make fun of others and raise one's voice, to decide over right and wrong, and to discuss other people and their business. Finally, it is inappropriate to emphasize one's reputation, to belittle the rest of the physicians and to praise only one's own virtue. Indeed, in actual life someone who has accidentally healed a disease, then stalks around with his head raised, shows conceit and announces that no one in the entire world could measure up to him. In this respect all physicians are evidently incurable.

Lao-tzu has said: When the conduct of men visibly reveals virtue, the humans themselves will reward it. If, however, men commit their virtues secretly, the spirits will reward them. When the conduct of men visibly reveals misdeeds, the humans themselves will take retribution. If, however, men commit their misdeeds secretly, the spirits will take retribution. When comparing these alternatives and the respective rewards which will be given in the time after this life and still during this life, how could one ever make a wrong decision?

Consequently physicians should not rely on their own excellence, neither should they strive with their whole heart for material goods. On the contrary, they should develop an attitude of goodwill. If they move on the right path concealed [from the eyes of their contemporaries], they will receive great happiness as a reward without asking for it. The wealth of others should not be the reason to prescribe precious and expensive drugs, and thus make the access to help more difficult and underscore one's own merits and abilities. Such conduct has to be regarded as contrary to the teaching of magnanimity [*chung-shu*].[20] The object is help. Therefore I enter into all the problems in such detail here. Whoever studies medicine should not consider [these problems] insignificant![21]□

Thirty years after Sun Szu-miao had composed this section in the *Ch'ien-chin fang,* he wrote the similarly voluminous work *Ch'ien-chin i-fang.* The 29th and 30th chapters were devoted to the practices of magic and the so-called techniques of interdiction. At the opening of the 29th chapter, Sun Szu-miao cited a brief ethics by the respective practitioners, evidently from an older shamanistic work. When and in what context it was compiled originally is not known. At the time he wrote his first book, Sun Szu-miao possibly already knew of this text and was influenced by it. The older text lacks the paradigmatic feature of Sun Szu-miao's own explanations of the ethics of physicians. In addition it does not emphasize elite groups and other aspects which were introduced by Sun Szu-miao. The unknown author addressed his colleagues rather than the public; as the following rendition of the text discloses, the author devoted himself largely to the need of his group for protection from their contemporaries and from the spirits.

□ *FIVE EXHORTATIONS*

First: not to kill; second: not to steal; third: not to live immorally; fourth: not to engage in perfidious talk; fifth: not to drink wine, nor to be envious.

TEN TYPES OF GOOD CONDUCT

First: to assist those who are in need and difficulties; second: to bury dead men and perished birds and animals which are found on the way; third: to respect demons and celestial beings; fourth: not to kill, nor injure anyone, and to develop a compassionate attitude; fifth: not to envy the rich and despise the poor; sixth: to preserve a temperate disposition; seventh: not to set value on the

20. This term combines two value terms of the Confucian social doctrine; a more literal rendition is "truthfulness toward the principles of one's own nature" (*chung*) and "benevolent application of these principles in regard to one's fellow men" (*shu*).

21. Chang Lu, *Ch'ien-chin fang yen-i.*

expensive and scorn the cheap; eighth: not to drink wine, nor eat meat or pungent foods; ninth: not to indulge in music or women; tenth: to keep one's disposition and character well-balanced, not to lapse alternately into a bad mood and then again into a good mood.

EIGHT TABOOS

First: to look at dead bodies; second: to look at blood from an execution; third: to look at processes of birth; fourth: to look at the six types of domestic animals when they give birth; fifth: to look at children in mourning and at people shedding tears; sixth: to embrace small children; seventh: to sleep with women; eighth: to speak with strangers about the practices.

FOUR RESTRICTIONS

First: It will not do to wear soiled, contaminated clothing. Communication with the spirits would thereby be prevented.

Second: It will not do to curse maliciously and to utter insults.

Third: It will not do to discuss fraudulent teachings with other people and to call on the saints in this connection.

Fourth: It will not do to drink wine, to eat meat, to kill or injure someone and not to live true to the right principles.

Then it says: It will not do to recite texts of interdiction at contaminated places.

Then it says: It will not do to perform interdictions with persons who do not believe in them.

Then: It will not do to impart the procedures of interdiction to outsiders.

Then: It will not do to hold texts of interdiction with impure hands.

Then: It will not do to make noise and to lark about with outsiders.

Then: It will not do to speak slightingly of the gods.

Then: It will not do to beat any of the six kinds of domestic animals or men in anger, neither will it do to ride in carts or on horses.

Whoever transgresses against three maxims out of the sum of those cited here will not succeed in the practices of interdiction. Whoever is able to avoid offences will bring on great success with his interdictions.[22] □

22. Sun Szu-miao, *Ch'ien-chin i-fang,* ch. 29, pp. 1a–1b.

A Confucian Response

Approximately one hundred-fifty years after Sun Szu-miao had developed his own instructions for medical ethics and had put them down in the *Ch'ien-chin fang*, Lu Chih (A.D. 754–805) expressed the view of a Confucian scholar in regard to both medicine as such and the group who practiced medicine independently as a means to earn money. Already in his young days Lu Chih had successfully passed the examinations for the career of civil servant, and graduated at the age of eighteen to a *chin-shih*. After some time spent in less important administrative positions, he finally received a key position in the Han-lin academy and became an intimate friend and adviser of the emperor. His political writings are known to posterity. Lu Chih can thus be considered a representative of the ruling class of his time. His views on medicine and its practice therefore carry special weight:

☐ Medicine is based on practiced humaneness [*jen-shu*]. The sentiments of the physicians are focused on living men; hence it is said: "Medicine is practiced humaneness." When someone suffers from a disease and seeks a cure, this is no less important than if someone facing death by fire or by drowning calls for help. Physicians are advised to practice humaneness and compassion. Without dwelling on [externals such as] tresses and a cap that fits, they have to hasten to the relief of him [who asks for it]. This is the proper thing to do. Otherwise accidents such as burning or drowning take place. How could a man who is guided by humaneness calmly tolerate such a happening?

Yet in many places there are physicians who make use of the needs of others and who appropriate their goods to themselves in a fraudulent way. This is a case of very diligent partisans of greed. How can this be reconciled with "practiced humaneness"? Very many have adopted this [frame of mind] and their deeds are by no means admirable. Why on earth are they not rewarded for it by misfortune?

Nowadays it can frequently be observed that the descendants of [good] physicians accumulate luxury, live in happiness and in splendor and are elected to the higher ranks. In the last instance this is yet another expression of a reward through heavenly principles. What need is there then to plan only for the profit which arises from an occasion and to then be considered a thief?

The attitude of humaneness and righteousness [*i*] is in contrast to the magic arts. The latter contradict the heavenly principles which are provided for living creatures. Whoever devotes himself to such [practices] cannot pass for an example."[23]□

I wish to comment on several points in this statement. In the first paragraph of this short essay Lu Chih indicates that medicine should be a matter of course for everyone who is endowed with an "attitude of humaneness," as indeed all men are, according to Mencius, who demonstrated this with his example of the well. The logical consequence of this thought is that the "primary" resources of medicine have to be distributed evenly among the population. In the second paragraph Lu Chih then points to those who practice medicine for money-making, and in this context he partially questions Sun Szu-miao's system of rewards. In casting doubt on the certainty that a higher power will impose a punishment on physicians for their fraudulent machinations, he adds again to the distrust which, according to his opinion, should be shown to these practitioners. In the third paragraph he argues accordingly that those who make use of medicine in the sense preferred by him will be richly reimbursed by society, not necessarily in their own but at least in the succeeding generation. In his conclusion he makes a very obvious critique of the Taoists' involvement with alchemy and magic. Sun Szu-miao was in fact numbered among those so involved.

It is remarkable in Lu Chih's statements that he does not show contempt for medicine as a resource, but merely for its practice as a profession. Notwithstanding observations of this nature on the part of a high level representative of the political hierarchy, authors throughout later centuries repeatedly sensed the need to increase the value of medicine in the face of orthodox Confucianism, and expressed this in the prefaces to their medical works. Such efforts were not limited to the group of physicians who remained outside the career of the Confucian examinations and the civil service. Among the Confucian scholars who tried to overcome the ideology of discredit directed at this field of activity were also those who dealt with medicine beyond the "domain of families," either because they had been appointed civil servants or

23. Lu Chih, *Lu Hsüan kung lun,* in Hsü Ch'un-fu, *Ku-chin i-t'ung ta-ch'üan,* ch. 3b, pp. 13a–13b.

because of their private interest. Thus the following example comes from a preface to a new edition of the classic on acupuncture and moxabustion, *Chia-i ching,* by Huang-fu Mi (A.D. 215–82). This was edited in the governmental office of publications by the well-known trio of civil servants, Kao Pao-heng, Sun Ch'i and Lin I, around A.D. 1092:

□ We have heard the following [information]: the scientific insight into heaven, earth and man is called "Confucian scholarship" [*ju*]. The scientific insight into heaven and earth but not into man is called "technology" [*chi*]. Medicine is referred to as the technology which concerns itself with the formulas for prescriptions [*fang-chi*], but is it not actually to be considered as one of the concerns of Confucian scholarship? Pan Ku has said in the introduction to the chapter *I-wen chih* [of his historical work on the earlier period of Han]: "The Confucian scholars assist man and the ruler. They act corresponding to *yin* and *yang* and clarify the teachings and the changes." This corresponds to the scientific insight into the principles of heaven, earth and men. We read further: "The scientists concerned with the formulas of prescriptions discuss the diseases until they advance to the origins of the government. They treat [the diseases] with a knowledge which equals that of public administration." If they did not gain insight into the secrets of heaven, earth *and* of men with their knowledge, how then could they approach the public administration?[24]□

Only a short time later, K'ou Tsung-shih formulated the following statement in his introductory sections to a work on *materia medica,* the *Pen-ts'ao yen-i,* in A.D. 1119:

□ The failure to cure [diseases] is based on six mistakes: the mistake of proceeding carelessly [at the treatment], the mistake of lacking trust, the mistake of missing a deadline, the mistake of not calling a physician, the mistake of failing to recognize the disease, and, finally, the mistake of not knowing the drugs. If but one of these mistakes is committed, it will be difficult to heal.

As becomes apparent, it is not only the fault of the physicians, but also the incorrect conduct of the patient which plays a role. If the physician is not guided by compassion [*tz'u*] and humaneness [*jen*] and the patient begins therefore to doubt and despise [the

24. Okanishi, *Sung i-ch'ien i-chi k'ao,* p. 238.

physician], these two types of conduct will certainly not be useful for any control over the disease. That is to say, by all means, a physician has to be guided by compassion and humaneness, otherwise he calls for misfortune. Under no circumstances is a patient to doubt and to despise [the physician], otherwise he [the patient] calls for misfortune.[25]□

K'ou Tsung-shih was a Confucian civil servant. Although not voluminous, his work occupies a significant position in the development of medical thinking in China and brought him the position of an "expert in the purchase of drugs" (and that probably in the imperial office of drugs at the court). For the first time a decided influence of neo-Confucian thinking on medicine can be traced in his work in the form of a "symbolic syncretism" which included Confucian, Taoist, and Buddhist elements.[26] It is this fact and the relationship of K'ou Tsung-shih to the Confucian bureaucratic system which make it clear why the author was able to discuss medical ethics in one or two sentences. Medical practice meant for him merely one of many duties arising from the Confucian values "compassion" and "humaneness," and in this he fully agrees with the demands of Lu Chih. K'ou Tsung-shih had no interest in giving a higher value to the freely practicing physicians, therefore one does not observe the numerous marginal instructions which Sun Szu-miao gave to his colleagues. As a civil servant K'ou Tsung-shih had to be intent on justifying his own medical activity.

*Chu Hsi's Stigmatization of Medicine
and Some Replies by Practitioners*

Ever since Chu Hsi (A.D. 1130–1200) had made his grave statements about medicine, everyone who brought a special interest to the subject was bound to feel an increased urge for such justifying statements, regardless of whether he practiced independently or was a scholar concerned with theories.

Chu Hsi, the outstanding philosopher of neo-Confucianism, annotated the classic Confucian authors of antiquity, and in this context made a value judgment on medicine which remained effective for centuries. In his *Analects* (*Lun-yü*) Confucius had ob-

25. K'ou Tsung-shih, *Pen-ts'ao yen-i,* ch. 1, p. 7.
26. Paul U. Unschuld, *Pen-ts'ao,* pp. 75–92; more explicitly, Ulrike Unschuld, "Traditional Chinese Pharmacology."

served: "The southerners have a saying: 'A man without persistence cannot become a sorcerer-physician [*wu-i*].' Good"[27]

The meta-statement contained in this known quotation can also be translated in the following manner, while adhering fully to the correct grammar: "A man without persistence can neither become a sorcerer [*wu*], nor a physician [*i*]." In the Western secondary literature both versions can be found. Thus R.G. Bridgman translated *wu-i* as the binominal term "*prêtre-médecin*"[28] in his essay on medicine in ancient China. James Legge, on the contrary, divided *wu* and *i*, and thus adopted the second version referred to.[29] He was followed in this by Joseph Needham who, in my opinion, was biased in his translation when he wrote: "he [i.e. Confucius] himself made a celebrated reference to them [i.e. the physicians], when he said that 'a man without persistence will never make a good magician [*wu*] or a good physician [*i*].' "[30]

Chu Hsi may have been the ancestor of this alternate version, because he explained the two parts separately: *wu* as sorcerers communicating with the supernatural, and *i* as physicians. As a corollary he wrote: "If it applies thus for such insignificant personnel [*chien-i*], [others] will not manage without persistence all the more."[31] At another place in the *Analects* of Confucius we read as follows: "Tzu Hsia has said: 'To be sure the petty teachings [*hsiao-tao*] also contain aspects which have to be considered, but whoever goes too far with this will be soiled. Therefore the high-minded does not occupy himself with them.' "[32] To this Chu Hsi wrote in his commentary: "By *hsiao-tao* we do not mean 'alien principles' [*i-tuan*] [as an earlier commentator had noted]. Hsiao-tao points also to 'teachings' [*tao-li*], but only to 'petty' ones [*hsiao*]. As for instance: agriculture, horticulture, medicine, prophecy, and all the other types of specialized work.'"[33]

From then on Chu Hsi's classification of medicine as "petty teaching" clung to medical practice like a stigma. Not only the independently practicing physicians objected to this classification, some criticism also came from Confucian circles. In order to

27. Lun-yü, XIII, 25, in James Legge, *The Chinese Classics,* vol. 1, p. 272.
28. Bridgman, "La médecine dans la Chine antique," p. 188.
29. Legge, *The Chinese Classics,* vol. 1, p. 272.
30. Needham, *Clerks and Craftsmen,* p. 264.
31. Chu Hsi, *Lun-yü chi-chu,* pp. 598–601.
32. Lun-yü, IX, 4, in Legge, *The Chinese Classics,* vol. 1, pp. 340–41.
33. Chu Hsi, *Chu-tzu ch'üan-shu,* ch. 19, p 23a.

summarize three direct reactions to Chu Hsi's statements, we have to advance somewhat further in time.

Around A.D. 1156 there lived a physician by the name of Hsü Ch'un-fu. He had studied medicine as a student of the well-known physician Wang Huan, and was later employed for a time as a civil servant at the imperial medical office. Hsü Ch'un-fu acquired an outstanding knowledge of medical literature and published a voluminous compendium, the *Ku-chin i-t'ung ta-ch'üan,* in which he summed up selected sections from earlier works beginning with the *Huang-ti nei-ching.* In the third chapter he collected various statements on the status of physicians in society, and added an independent section in which he took up Chu Hsi's interpretation of the term *wu-i:*

☐ *SORCERER-PHYSICIANS* [*WU-I*]

In the *Analects* [of Confucius] we read: "A man without persistence cannot become a sorcerer-physician."

Confucius here expressed his regret that a man without persistence could not excel. It is a significant statement. Master Chu [Hsi] wrote the following commentary to it: "Sorcerers [*wu*] converse with demons and spirits; the decision over death and life is entrusted to the physicians [*i*]." By dividing [the term *wu-i*] in two parts, [Chu Hsi] did not proceed correctly.

The teaching of medicine has its origin in Shen-nung and has been explained by Huang-ti. [The latter] composed the *Nei-ching su-wen* for the examination of specific diseases and the use of particular drugs. This work is called the "magnificent codex of a saint" and it serves to assist the population in its fate. How could anyone speak simultaneously [of this teaching of medicine] and of the group of sorcerers even within the span of a single day?

Among those who have taken up the study of medicine, naturally we have to distinguish between the "sophisticated" and the "uncouth" [persons]. Therefore the designations given to them vary. Those who practice medicine in an "ingenious" way are called "enlightened physicians" [*ming-i*]; those who have an excellent command over medicine are called "good physicians" [*liang-i*]; those who bring a long life to the emperor and protect the ministers [from diseases] are called "state physicians" [*kuo-i*]; those who perform their work in an unskilled manner and to whom the principles [of medicine] remain hidden are called "common physicians" [*yung-i*]; those, finally, who beat the drums and perform dances, who recite prayers and prepare sacrifices [to ward off] suffering and diseases, are called "sorcerer-physicians" [*wu-i*].

[Explanation in small print:] We speak of sorcerer-physicians because these people replace medicine by magic. It is apparent that those who join the sorcerers possess no knowledge of the principles of medicine and of drugs. When therefore the southerners spoke of "sorcerer-physicians," they referred to these [practitioners]. Nowadays in the south they are called *tuan-kung t'ai-pao* or even *yeh-hsing pu-shih*. In the north the current designation is *shih-p'o*. Although these people merely display empty ostentation, they nevertheless have to remain persistent even in this. How much more so does this apply to other people![34]□

Lai Fu-yang (fl. A.D. 1596?) wrote in the preface to a new edition of the *Nan-yang huo-jen shu* by Chu Kung (fl. A.D. 1088):

□ If medical practice is based on deception, it is to be considered low. If medicine is practiced on the principles of veracity [*chen*], it is not to be considered low. If a person's knowledge of medicine is applied only to his own body, this is petty [*hsiao*]. If the application [of a person's medical knowledge] is extended over all mankind, this is not petty![35]□

Chang Wei-jen expresses himself in a similar manner in another preface to the same work:

□ Ever since Chu Tzu-yang [that is Chu Hsi] classified medicine as "petty teaching" [*hsiao-tao*], the Confucians have attached little value to it. They "put it aside" and do not speak of it any more. Yet not to speak about it also means not to practice it. All those who still practice medicine and become renowned by it have failed in a Confucian career. Yet if [the Confucians themselves] fall ill one day, they will still have to consult those [practitioners] who are so uncomfortable to them. . . . In most cases those who have entered upon a Confucian career do not know anything about medicine.[36]□

34. Hsü Ch'un-fu, *Ku-chin i-t'ung ta-ch'üan*, ch. 3b, pp. 5b–6a.
35. Okanishi, *Sung i-ch'ien i-chi k'ao*, p. 626.
36. Ibid.

Confucian Scholar Physicians Enter the Debate

In Chang Kao, *tzu* name: Chi-ming, (fl. A.D. 1210), the author
of a medical compendium (*I-shuo*) which contains a detailed
section about medical ethics, we encounter a Confucian who practiced medicine as a "Confucian physician" (*ju-i*) and who evidently descended from a family with a medical tradition. In A.D.
1207 Chiang Ch'ou composed the following epilogue for the
I-shuo, in which he explains the social framework in which the
group of the *ju-i* found itself:

□ [Chang] Chi-ming is a Confucian scholar. He has compiled the
present collection of statements [by earlier physicians] in order to
make them known to his own time. People frequently laugh at
him, because he engages in such a "technical activity" [*chi*].
They are not aware that he thereby manifests the disposition of a
true man of letters! If all who practice medicine in this world
adopted the disposition of Chi-ming, they would be good physicians [*liang-i*], even if they merely possessed the status of common physicians [*yung-i*]. Of course, those who devote themselves
[to medicine] with the aspirations of a broker, will be but common
physicians, even if [from the point of view of their skill] they
should be considered good physicians. How much more does this
apply to those who are already common by their very personal
disposition! . . .

Chi-ming's practiced humaneness expressed itself in [helping
others] to treat their pains by themselves in case of illness and not
to have to give themselves up to the malpractices of common
physicians. How in the face of this fact can anyone consider the
present collection of statements [by earlier physicians] as "technical activity" and make fun of it? Chi-ming took over the secret
traditions of his great-uncle. Because of his attitude and the practice of this "technical activity" he can be considered a good
example of the Confucian physicians [*ju-i*]. For the same reason
he has successfully passed the examinations of the second class
and found a position with the civil service.[37] □

Chiang Ch'ou's belief that it is the aim of a Confucian physician to help men to treat themselves without having to abandon
themselves to "common practitioners," is worthy of separate in-

37. Ibid., p. 1114.

vestigation. In Western secondary literature we find the term *yung-i* for the most part rendered by derogatory terms, such as "quack," "charlatan," etc. In doing this we adopt the value judgment of the Confucians. By the same token we could exchange the values and maintain that an expert such as Sun Szu-miao was a "good physician," whereas it is rather the Confucian leisure time physicians who resemble "quacks." In the debate on medical ethics however, we do not deal with objective norms of good and bad, but with the influence of such value judgments on the distribution of resources. Just as Sun Szu-miao denounced the "primary" resources of the remaining physicians as insufficient in order to increase the "secondary" resources of his own core group of "Great Physicians" (*ta-i*), authors like Chiang Ch'ou criticized the "primary" resources of all the "common physicians" in order to expand the control of their group of Confucian physicians over "secondary" resources.

Already Chiang Ch'ou's preface conveys the conflict which was unavoidable for the *ju-i*. Although they endeavored to put medical resources under the control of the Confucians, they already formed a special group of experts within the larger group of Confucianism. Their surplus in resources had to arouse suspicion and thus called for justification. Accordingly the group of Confucian physicians was driven into a two-sided conflict, first against its own larger group and second against the independently practicing physicians who were outside of Confucianism.[38]

Along these same lines Chang Kao formulated his ethics very differently from most authors who devoted themselves to this topic. Under the title "retributions for medical services" (*"I-kung pao-ying"*) he placed the practice of medicine in a striking relationship to Buddhist ideas of rewards and punishments by the powers of another world. His ethics is expressed in twelve anec-

---

38. In our society a process takes place between three groups, physicians, psychiatrists and psychologists, which is in many respects similar. On the one hand within the medical profession the psychiatrists guarantee that psychiatry remains in the hands of the "physicians." On the other hand, as experts in the medical profession, the psychiatrists have to struggle for "primary" and "secondary" resources with their colleagues who are specialized in other areas. The process of professionalization which brought them into a twofold conflict with their own mother group and the psychologists, the technical rivals and non-physicians, evidently closely resembles the process of professionalization in pre-republican China.

dotes, which present exemplary instances of good and bad with the respective consequences. The methodical structure of this cycle of twelve is selected in such a manner as to make clear to the reader what a praiseworthy and precious resource medical practice constitutes, since it enables one to gain merit through assistance offered to ill fellow humans which will be noted in another world. By means of a praiseworthy example of an evidently Confucian physician in his second story the author establishes a potential trust relationship with this group, and then makes a transition to the decadence of morals in his own time with the third story. The following seven stories all contain discreditable instances of medical practice, which are followed by punishment in each case. Not until the final two anecdotes is the potential of trust in physicians once more raised by means of exemplary conduct. Chang Kao limited his explanations to the following central dimensions of ethics: greed vs. unselfish help, exploitation of sexual opportunities, conscientiousness in practice, and the problem of abortions.

□ *REWARD FOR MEDICAL SERVICES*

The scholar Hsü—When Hsü Shu-wei was still young in years, he had already begun praying for success in his future examinations for the career of civil servant. One night a spirit appeared to him in his dream uttering the following words: "It is your wish to be successful in the examinations for the career of civil servant. For this merits are needed which are recorded in another world [*yin-te*]!" [Hsü] Shu-wei thought to himself that his family was poor and had no influence and that only medicine would be appropriate [to meet the demands of the spirit in his dream]. Thereafter he concentrated on the manuals of the medical prescriptions and after intensive study he became fully conversant with their secrets. Everyone was eager to see him, irrespective of their high or low rank. The number of those whose lives were saved grew unceasingly, and Hsü's fame increased steadily. Then the spirit reappeared to him in his dream and spoke the following verse:

> Drugs show hidden effects,
> There is a place between Ch'en and Lou;
> In the hall a complete success,
> Call six, results in five.

In the same year Hsü passed the examinations for the title of the *chin-shih* in the sixth place. In the list of grades earned by the graduates Ch'en Tsu-yen was named before him, Lou Ts'ai after him. A remark was added there that as a sign of favor Hsü was advanced one place in the list of rating, as if he held the fifth place. He received the title of civil servant and returned. Every word of the dream had come true. So fare those who deliver others from their diseases and support them in need!

The physician Nieh, a good scholar—In Hua-t'ing, in the district of I, there lived a capable physician by the name of Nieh Ts'ung-chih. One day when the wife of the officer of the district, one born Li, fell ill and approached death, Nieh treated her and cured her. The woman Li was fair and seductive. She was smitten by his conduct. One day when her husband had travelled to a neighboring district, the woman Li had [the physician Nieh] called under the pretext that she had fallen ill. When he arrived, she said to him: "I was on the point of being entered into the lists of afterlife, when I came back to life due to your help. Even if I consider all the things of this world, nothing will suffice to pay back your good deed. Therefore I wish to offer you my body in my bedroom." Nieh was startled and ran away tormented by apprehensions. On the eve of the same day Mrs. Li ventured still another attempt and went to him richly ornamented. But Nieh struggled free [from her] and ran away again. After that she desisted from her approaches and no one else heard a word of this.

More than one year later Huang Ching-kuo, an officer of investigation, fell ill. A messenger of the underworld pulled him down for a hearing. Later, however, he was sent back again from there to the bank of a river. [In the underworld] Huang Ching-kuo had observed a prison-warden who dragged along a woman, cut open her body and cleansed her entrails. A Buddhist priest who stood nearby explained to him: "This is the wife of your colleague, the officer such-and-such. She had plans to have illegitimate intercourse with the physician Nieh. Nieh however did not agree to it, we can truly call him a good scholar. Originally his life had been timed for sixty years, yet because of his merits, which were recorded in another world, it was prolonged for twelve years. Moreover in the following generations his sons and his grandsons will be appointed civil servants. This woman's life, however, was shortened for as many years as Nieh's life was prolonged. In addition her entrails were cleansed, in order to remove the corruption!''

Ching-kuo was a close acquaintance of Nieh. After he had ascended back to the [upper] world, he visited him secretly, in order to ask him about the matter. Nieh was startled and said: ''This is a question of completely private conversations, of which so far no one has heard anything at all. Moreover, I was alone in this room when she came here that evening. Only the woman and I knew of it. How did you find out of this affair?'' Ching-kuo told him everything. After Nieh had died, one of his sons passed the examinations for the career of civil servant. His grandson T'u-nan became a civil servant in the precinct of Han-chung. . . . He composed a poem of several hundred words, to reveal the virtue [of his grandfather]. This poem, however, will be omitted here.

The use of fradulent methods to deprive others is widespread—Wang Chu-an who held the title of a *hsiu-ts'ai* suffered for a long time from hemorrhoids. Now he found out that there was a capable practitioner [*shan-kung*] in Hsiao-shan. As he did not have the means to send for him, he rented a boat and himself travelled from Wu-ch'eng to Ch'ien-t'ang. There he moved into a quiet inn. He dispatched someone to invite the physician; the latter crossed the river to get to him. When he caught sight of the patient, he set about preparing the drugs for the cure. And he said: ''Allow me to put an end to the origin [of the ailment] within five days. At first we will let the colon protrude several inches with the aid of a drug. With a further drug we will cleanse it. Then we will slowly constrict the hemorrhoids with a medical thread, until they will in two days fall off at about the size of a peach. Thereafter further drugs will have to be taken as an after-treatment, until a complete recovery is attained after several days.'' In the beginning that practitioner did not display any bad qualities. Yet once he had accomplished the protrusion of the colon, he suddenly began to negotiate material rewards. The patient was fully aware of his dependence and gave away everything he possessed. Only then did the aforesaid practitioner prepare himself to carry out the treatment to its end.

And a further example: Chou Chin from Yü-shan had been transferred to the post of an official in the nation's capital. For some time he had been suffering from a fractured testicle. A druggist spoke to him: "That can be cured in no time, if I receive 10,000 cash in money and three bundles of double-threaded silk as a reward!" They betook themselves into a room and [the druggist] inserted a needle for an acupuncture treatment. The ailment was thus terminated. Chou was highly pleased and the druggist received the desired amount of money and material and left. Yet already half a month later the old ailment reappeared. [Chou] conducted a search for that specific physician, yet he was not seen any more. Several of the exemplary figures in antiquity occupied themselves with medicine and the art of prophecy. Among the present-day physicians all are ardently concerned with fame and gain. In general they make use of fraudulent methods and their moral principle is robbery. There is no longer a difference between them and the bandits who move along with a sword! These two examples have caught my attention; I record them here, in order to warn this world.

Hsü Lou-t'ai—In the eighth year of the title of reign *shao-hsing* [A.D. 1138] Hsü Lou-t'ai and Sun Ta-lang from Tang-t'u, two physicians of external medicine, treated a rich man by the name of Chiang Shun-ming, from La-shan in the district of Li-shui, for an ulcer on his back. Besides 25 *liang* of silver they demanded 300,000 cash in money as a reward. The patient refused to pay them this sum. Thereupon the physicians infused a small amount of a drug wrapped in paper into the wound which aggravated the ailment to such a point that the patient died. Not even a year had passed, when Hsü [Lou-t'ai] fell ill with a fever. He cried unceasingly and said: "Shun-ming! Don't beat me!" After a few days he died. His son could not marry any more and thus Hsü's medical knowledge died out.

Fu Chu-chiao—In Hsüan-ch'eng there lived a man by the name of Fu Chu-chiao in the town of Fu-li. He treated ulcers, but he deliberately neglected to proceed with the necessary care. If the wounds of his patients had originally been free from poison, then it developed because of his drugs. Finally a messenger from the underworld came to him unexpectedly. He wore a yellow coat and showed him a note in his hand, adding: "An official in the underworld searches for you" and he hit his back with a heavy cane. Fu cried out loudly with pain and the messenger clad in yellow said: "See, see, you too seem to know pain." Immediately a great ulcer developed on Fu Chu-chiao's back and he died.

The physician Lu from Shui-yang—In the district of Kuan-nei
in Hsüan-ch'eng there lived the physician Lu Yang, whose *tzu*
name was I-jo, in a village by the name of Shui-yang. His skill
had made him famous. During the title of reign *chien-yen* [A.D.
1127–30] the wife of the supervisor of scriptures in the Han-lin
academy fell ill, because she had been terrified during a flight
from robbers. Lu treated her erroneously with *hsiao ch'ai-hu* decoction and killed her with this.

Mrs. Li's son from Kao-shun in Li-shui fell ill with consumption. They had Lu come, who devoted himself attentively to the
case. Yet even before his efforts showed success, he went out to
drink in the houses of pleasure. In the patient's house he demanded money and indulged in wine and dainty foods, as if he
were not in the least concerned with the fate of the patient. In the
end he had Mrs. Li's son take a number of hard pills which killed
him.

In the ninth year of *shao-hsing* [A.D. 1139] Lu fell ill unexpectedly. He cried out: "Chu I-jen and Li Liu-lang stop beating me! I
will go on my own account!" Within ten days he died.

*A blind Buddhist priest who practices medicine receives a
reward*—In I-chou there lived a Buddhist priest by the name of Fa
Ch'eng, with the *tzu* name Wu-chu, who practiced medicine. He
had been blind from his youth and no conceivable treatment had
been successful. Nevertheless he repeated the name of Kuan-yin
day and night. Fifteen years passed in this manner, when he heard
the Boddhisattva call him in a dream. Yet it felt as if his legs had
been tied down; he could not approach her. The Boddhisattva
spoke to him with a sigh: "In an earlier generation you were a
Moxa-master [*chiu-shih*]. Through incorrect treatments you dam-
aged the eyes of your fellow humans. In your present life you
receive the requital for it; there is no way out. Yet owing to your
upright disposition I have pity on you, and I will see to it that
clothes and food will be at your disposal in abundance." Thereafter she brought forth rich treasures with both hands from her
robe and gave them to the priest. After this he woke up. Henceforth his medical practice drew large crowds. He always had a
sufficient amount of clothing and his poorbox was always amply
filled. Thus he became more than seventy years old.

An abortion is followed by a requital in the end—In the nation's capital there lived a woman by the name of Pai. She was

endowed with good looks and everyone called her Pao Mu-tan. She earned her living by the sale of medicaments for abortion. One day her head started to ache unexpectedly, it increased its size by the day. Renowned physicians treated her, yet not one of them was able to heal her. After some time she developed running sores with such bad odours that one could not bear it any longer. Every night [Mrs. Pai] screamed so loudly that it had to be heard near and far. In the end she said to her relatives: "Burn my prescriptions for abortions which I have collected." To her children she said with a warning: "Take an oath that you will not continue this trade." Her son replied: "Mother, with the aid of this trade you have helped our family to gain a reputation. Why should we give it up?" She answered as follows: "Every night I dream that hundreds of small children suck at my brain. For this reason I have such strong pains that I have to scream. All this is the requital for my destroying the fruit of the womb with strong medicines." After this she died.

Tuan Ch'eng-wu—Tuan Ch'eng-wu from I-hsing possessed outstanding medical abilities. Yet he was very greedy, and whoever was not very well-to-do could not call on him. The nobleman Ts'ui Chung-hui from Ch'ang-shu wished to see him, but Tuan declined. Not until [Sir Ts'ui] asked the *shou*-official Liang Shang-shu from P'ing-chiang to invite [the physician], did he come. When [Tuan Ch'eng-wu] returned from P'ing-chiang, it so happened accidentally that a rich man fell ill and requested medical treatment of him. Tuan said: "This disease can easily be cured by various boiled medicaments. Yet I will only make this possible if I receive 500,000 cash in money." The family of the patient was at first only willing to concede one half of this reward. Whereupon the physician gathered up his clothes and left, so that they finally responded to his demands. In addition to it the family offered 50 *liang* of silver for the drugs, yet Tuan expected a profit of 100 *liang* and did not fetch the drugs for the treatment [until he had received the amount]. After several days the recovery set in and [Tuan] returned home toward the west with his gain. On the way he dreamt one night of a messenger from the underworld in a red coat who spoke to him: "You practice medicine and enrich yourself by it beyond all bounds. According to divine opinion no charitable disposition is expressed in such conduct. Therefore a command was issued that you receive twenty blows on your back with a heavy cane." Whereupon [the messenger] commanded his companions to seize the physician and to whip him. Tuan woke up and felt pains on his back. He called a servant to check the reason for it. Traces of the blows could be found on his back. Tuan returned home humbly and died shortly thereafter.

The grand king Pao-chün—The daughter of a family of Ming-chou had celebrated her wedding and now returned to her parents. Yu-lan, a concubine, followed some other servants into the back yard to fetch vegetables. Suddenly she became indisposed and fell to the ground. From her mouth came unintelligible words, as if she had been possessed. The others supported her and helped her to her room, where she came to herself half a day later. Asked for the reason [for her collapse] she told the following story: "Death is certain for me! In my former life I was an eye-doctor at Hopei. An old unmarried woman lived there in a village. Once when she suffered from an inflammation of the eyes, I had an evil interest in her possessions and killed her with the aid of a drug. Then I took everything that lay stored up in her apartment and no one ever heard about it. Yet the old woman reported it to the god of the easternmost of the holy mountains and a command was issued to seize and punish me. However, the years allotted to me had not yet expired, so that I could not be seized.

"Twenty years ago I finally died and was reborn in this district here. The old woman had not yet forgotten her vengeful hatred. Once more she left the underworld and ascended again to the god of the easternmost of the holy mountains. The ruler there had pity on her. He selected a strong helper and sent him with an official letter into all the districts of the empire to search for me. He had almost completed his mission, when he came here and asked to be admitted to our city. Upon the request of the guard at the gates [the helper] presented the note [of the particular god]. Yet he received the following reply: 'This summons has been signed by Ch'eng Huang. In our city however matters are settled by the grand king Pao-chün. Ch'eng Huang does not have any right to enter here.' He dismissed the messenger and did not grant him entry into the city.

"The messenger and the old woman set out again and hid thirty miles outside the city under a high bridge. Several days passed, when another ghost came from the west and likewise stopped at the bridge, entering into a conversation with the messenger of the underworld. The [newly arrived] ghost said: 'At present I am serving Pao-chün as a courier. and am just returning from the temple Chu-shan in Tung-t'ing, where I had to deliver a note. What a chance to have met here! I wish you to follow me on my way. Then we will ask the guard at the city gates to grant you entry.' The two thanked him very much and were thus finally admitted into our city. Immediately they set out for the palace of Pao-chün and showed him the proclamation. When Pao-chün saw it, he asked: 'Is this not a proclamation of Ch'eng Huang! How did you enter here?' The messenger reported the entire event true to the facts. Pao-chün called in his own messenger and said to him: 'Together with [these two here] I will send you alone to carry out the search.' The messenger consented and the three left [the palace] together. For several days they were not successful. One evening in mid-autumn they heard an old woman recite the following song in an alley, while burning incense: 'There is a girl in this and this house who follows a bridal procession, etc.' Whereupon the old woman [who had been looking for me] rejoiced and exclaimed: 'The foe can be seized!' Hastily they ran to the described dwelling, but there the guardian spirit refused them entry. Therefore they hid in the back yard. At that very place they recognized me then as the person who had been recorded in the lists of the other world and whom they had set out to capture. There is no possibility of evading the guilt of my former life.''

The people in the house wanted to send for a sorcerer to help her. Yet the aforesaid concubine allowed no time to pass. She seized a knife and put out both of her eyes and died.

A physician refuses a sexual reward—During the reign period *hsüan-ho* [A.D. 1119–25] there lived a scholar who had been suffering from a disease for a number of years. No treatment had been able to afford him any cure. Now there was a capable physician by the name of Ho Ch'eng. The wife [of the sick scholar] had him called to her private rooms and said to him: ''For a long time my husband has been suffering from a disease. We have already mortgaged almost all our possessions and there is nothing left to balance the cost of the medical treatment and the drugs. I am therefore willing to offer my own body as payment.''

The physician declined with a serious countenance and retorted: ''Dear woman, how dare you speak in this manner! Set your mind at rest, I will perform a successful treatment, yet I cannot accept that you soil us both with such an [offer]. If but one outsider found out about this, not only would my treatment and

my drugs remain without success, I would also be punished by
men and spirits." Shortly thereafter he had cured the husband.
One night Ho Ch'eng dreamt of a spirit who led him into a temple
before a judge. "Your treatments and your drugs are successful,"
the latter said to him, "you did not exploit a situation of need to
satisfy your sexual desires with the wife of a free man. Therefore
the High Lord has issued the command to reward you with 50,000
cords of money and the position of a civil servant!" A few months
had hardly passed, when the imperial prince fell ill. The governmental physicians were not able to treat him successfully and a
proclamation was issued to all the physicians in the country.
Ch'eng responded to this proclamation and with a preparation of a
drug he brought about the cure. He was rewarded for this with
3,000 cords of money from the court. From this time on his
medical practice was very successful. In the capital he was called
"Mr. Ho, the expert in the office of medicine."

A physician with the intention to help men—Physicians should
remember: "When another person is ill, it is as though I myself
[am ill]." When a physician is called for relief, he should respond
speedily and without delay. Even if someone asks only for medicaments, [the physician] is to give them to him immediately without asking about his social status and his wealth. Those who have
made it their very special cause to help men will be granted
protection for this from another world. Those, however, who
exploit the needs of others and who enrich themselves on purpose
show an attitude lacking all humaneness. Therefore the underworld predestines misfortune for them.

In my neighborhood lived a capable physician by the name of
Chang Yen-ming. When Buddhist or Taoist priests, destitute
scholars, soldiers or poor people asked him for drugs, he did not
accept any money from anyone. On the contrary, he even presented these people with money and rice! When someone came
and asked him to visit the sick, he responded to it, no matter how
poor [these people] were. When well-to-do people asked for drugs
with money, he did not ask for the sum and always gave out too
great an amount of drugs in the hope the disease would thereby be
cured. He never had any intention of letting rich people come
again to bring still more money.

If someone suffered from a very serious disease, he still gave
out good drugs in order to relieve his heart. After the specific
patient's death he would not accept any money. I have lived with

him for a long time and know him very well. He practiced medicine without ever speaking of money. He could be labelled an outstanding man among physicians.

One day a great fire broke out in the city. Everything burnt and stood in thick smoke. Only his dwelling house was spared. One year, when the area was hit by a serious catastrophe to cattle, only his stables remained untouched by it. Thus the gods protected him! His sons studied and great presents were in store for them. Two or three of his grandsons lived in plenty and were handsome and healthy. They too were provided for richly by providence.

Many incur the loss of such favors because they have made material things their sole concern. What they thereby gain is always insufficient to balance the real loss. They cannot serve their colleagues as an example.[39]□

In a preface to a fourteenth century edition of the *Mai-ching*, a classic by Wang Hsi (A.D. 210–85), concerned with the theory of pulse diagnosis, we encounter the frequently expressed effort to raise the value of medicine by a reference to obvious parallels with the basic values and principles of Confucianism. This preface, appearing in A.D. 1327, states:

□ The Confucian teaching has made humaneness and righteousness the guiding principle and has created a network of various firm relationships in society so that people do not violate the penal or the civil law.

The medical teaching has made an attitude of humaneness the guiding principle and lends a helping hand against suffering and disease, so that people are saved from early death and physical need. Therefore the *Su-wen* and the *Nan-ching* of medicine are to the six classics of Confucianism as outside is to inside. All these works express the attitude of the sages in antiquity to render an advantage to the later generations in this world.[40]□

Doubts Are Voiced by Scholars
Concerning the Confucian Attitude
towards Medicine

There is one passage by Ko Ch'ien-sun (fl. A.D. 1348), in the preface to his work *Shih-yao shen-shu*, which is difficult to compare with the statements which have been given up to now. Ko

39. Chang Kao, *I-shuo*, ch. 10, pp. 31a–39a.
40. Okanishi, *Sung i-ch'ien i-chi k'ao*, p. 132.

Ch'ien-sun was the son of Ko Ying-lei. In his youth the latter had prepared himself for the career of civil servant, but the downfall of the Sung dynasty thwarted his plans. Thus he studied, as an alternative, the literature on prescriptions which his family possessed and became a known physician and writer who spread the teachings current during the time of the Chin and Yüan dynasties. His son Ko Ch'ien-sun is described to us as a man of exceptionally strong build who turned at first to martial arts. But later on he studied and acquired some knowledge in the *yin-yang* philosophy of nature, in astronomy and in other areas. Yet he too did not succeed in entering the career of civil servant; he failed the required examinations several times. So he decided to take up his father's medical career, although, as his biographers tell us, he found little pleasure in treating unknown patients.

The passage from his preface which appears below is worthy of our attention mainly because the author acquaints us with a type of "primary" medical resources which differs from that of the Confucians or of Sun Szu-miao. Ko Ch'ien-sun emphasizes knowledge originating from extensive clinical experience as opposed to that assimilated from literature. He argues in the manner of practicing experts; that is, not until the basic theoretical knowledge has been elaborated by practical experience will the desired success be attained. He distinguishes himself further from the Confucian medical doctors by declaring the realm of the supernatural as the origin of his resources, instead of establishing them in Confucian-backed philosophies of nature.

Like Sun Szu-miao, Ko Ch'ien-sun was a independently practicing physician. But in contrast to Sun Szu-miao, who advocated the interests of professionalization held by the core group of "Great Physicians," Ko Ch'ien-sun's statements rely solely on individual interest. Ko Ch'ien-sun measured his own infallibility by the product he created; the idea of shifting from an outcome evaluation to a process evaluation was obviously foreign to him:

☐ From my youth on I have studied and practiced medicine. I have tested prescriptions and examined pulses for over thirty years. Everywhere in the country I have extensively increased my knowledge. Yet all the uses of drugs to treat diseases, made solely according to the descriptions of others by word of mouth and in writing, still do not equal the toilsome sacrifice day and night at the side of a sickbed.

In my later years I encountered a man [unknown to me] and stayed with him for three months. He had a very profound understanding of medical principles; he had mastered the prescriptions and pulse-rates in all their details. Whenever he used medicaments, it resembled the shooting of arrows. Not one would have missed its aim. I told myself that this must be a person of supernatural abilities and asked him to become my teacher. He handed me a small volume of wondrously effective prescriptions. From a closer examination it became apparent that some were composed of a great number [of ingredients], others again only of three or four [single drugs]. I had witnessed with my own eyes how each single one of them proved its effectiveness in the patients. For me this gift represented the "longed-for rain after an extended period of drought; the rising of a bright moon during a march in dark night"! So much had my senses been enlightened.

Then I returned to Wu and every use [of the named prescriptions] was successful. They always were immediately effective. Thus I became convinced that these wondrously effective prescriptions were fit to be printed.[41] □

Tai Liang (A.D. 1317–83) lived at about the same time as Ko Ch'ien-sun. He had an extensive knowledge, which included the classic, historical and non-official literature. In addition to this Tai Liang had intensively studied medicine, prophecy, Buddhism, and Taoism. He had originally planned to prepare for the examinations necessary for the career of civil servant. Yet he abandoned this project and focused thereafter on the study of antique literature and poetry. During the title of reign *chih-cheng* (A.D. 1341– 67), due to a recommendation, he finally received a title as a Confucian scholar for his extensive knowledge and his specific accomplishments in both areas. The downfall of the Yüan dynasty forced his retirement in the south of the country. Yet the first emperor of the Ming dynasty sought him out and offered him a position as a civil servant at court. Tai Liang pleaded an old ailment as a pretext and refused the appointment.

In his short contribution to medicine, Tai Liang advocates the view that the deterioration of medical practice in comparison to much earlier times can be found in the Confucians' disrespect for physicians. He concludes that it was this Confucian policy of

---

41. Ko Ch'ien-sun, *Shih-yao shen-shu* (preface by Ko Ch'ien-sun, pp. 3a–3b), in Ch'eng Yung-p'ei, *Liu-li chai i-shu shih-chung*.

rejection of medical practice which encouraged dilettantism on the one side, and the turn away from the old principles and toward the ''new'' on the other. Tai Liang was able to adopt the values which the Confucians had used to justify their attitude. But he expressed exactly the contrary in an almost ironical formulation of the problem.

□ Medicine directs its attention to living men; in this it closely resembles our Confucianism. Yet since the period of T'ang it has been listed in the histories of the dynasties under the sections ''technical skills'' [*chi-i*] and we Confucians do not therefore deem it worthy of our pursuit. Today's physicians recite only the firmly established opinion of one school and preserve certain formulas of prescriptions, and rejoice in the fact that they have accidentally ''hit'' on a disease. For a long time they have ceased to carrry out thorough examinations and they do not explore the insights of the holy ones and the exemplary men of antiquity, in order to understand the interaction between *yin-yang* and creation. Moreover they neglect to carry out a comprehensive study of literature and to adopt the most diverse interpretations which could be of use in the discussion of the specific circumstances of a treatment. In extreme cases they even go so far as to completely disregard the old prescriptions and to adhere to interpretations which they themselves have invented. In this manner they deceive one another and much suffering is the consequence. Does this express the generous intention of the holy ones and the exemplary men; that is, to show compassion and benevolence to the population?[42]□

An occurrence similar to that experienced by Ko Ch'ien-sun (cited above) happened to a man by the name of Han Mao (fl. A.D. 1522). He too had prepared for a career as a Confucian civil servant and had then failed the very lowest examinations. In his disappointment he is said to have set out for the O-mei mountains to devote himself to the study of medicine. In a preface which Han Mao wrote to his work *Han-shih i-t'ung* there appears the doubt as to whether the Confucian ethos of a ''comprehensive education,'' that is to say, of the equal distribution of resources, could be made real at all:

42. Hsü Ch'un-fu, *Ku-chin i-t'ung ta-ch'üan,* ch. 3b, p. 9a.

☐ The Confucians of the Sung time said: "Every descendent of man unquestionably has to have some medical knowledge!"; moreover it has been reported: "Whoever does not work as a good minister, can at least work as a good physician." How deplorable that men cannot be equally capable in everything!⁴³☐

In A.D. 1522 a man by the name Yü Pien composed a preface to a supplementary work of the *I-shuo* by Chang Kao, the *Hsü i-shuo*. In a slightly modified way Yü Pien here cited the first of Han Mao's phrases, which is included in the above cited text, in order to speak for the group of the Confucian medical scholars:

☐ The people of the Ch'i and Liang time used to say: "Only those who understand the art of medicine [*i-shu*] can be called children who fulfill their duties toward their parents." That was an exaggeration. The Confucian scholars of the Sung time said: "Whoever leaves the cure of diseases to common physicians [*yung-i*] neither possesses compassion, nor does he fulfill his duties toward his parents. The knowledge of medicine is indispensable in the assistance of one's relatives [*shih-ch'in*]!" This is a clear statement.

The renowned physicians of former times, such as Chen Ch'üan,⁴⁴ Hsü Chih-ts'ang,⁴⁵ Li Ming-chih [see below], and Chu Yen-hsiu [see below], all started to practice medicine because their mothers fell ill. In persistent study they devoted themselves to the truly significant and explored the subtle secrets. It seems that there is no area in which the high-minded could not use his disposition.⁴⁶☐

This text is a remarkable testimony to the efforts toward professionalization among Confucian medical scholars. It asserted

43. Han Mao, *Han-shih i-t'ung*, ch. 1, p. 4b, in Ch'eng Yung-p'ei, *Liu-li chai i-shu shih-chung*.
44. Chen Ch'üan (A.D. 541?–643) and his brother Chen Li-yen are known as authors of medical works on drugs and other areas. They are said to have turned to the study of medicine after their mother had fallen ill. Cf. *Chiu T'ang-shu*, PNP, ch. 191, p. 15702.
45. Hsü Chih-ts'ang, a physician from the Sui time (A.D. 581–618), had an ancestor to whom the following saying is attributed: "The children of men have to taste the food [before the parents eat it] and they have to pay heed to [their] medicaments. How could someone who is not in command of the medical prescriptions be considered satisfactorily fulfilling his responsibilities as a child?" Cf. *Sui-shu*, PNP, ch. 78, p. 11961.
46. Okanishi, *Sung i-ch'ien i-chi k'ao*, p. 1114.

simultaneously that on the one hand it is not necessary for every man to possess medical knowledge, while on the other hand one should not entrust oneself to "common physicians." There remains then the Confucian physician as an alternative, who possesses the highest moral standard, since he considers medicine as assisting his relatives (*shih-ch'in*). Although Yü Pien limits himself in his statement to indications, we again recognize the double-edged conflict in which the *ju-i* were involved, to which I have alluded in connection with the preface by Chiang Ch'ou (see above, p. 43).

Among the exemplary physicians, Yü Pien enumerated Li Ming-chih (i.e., Li Kao, A.D. 1180–1251) and Chu Yen-hsiu (i.e., Chu Chen-heng, A.D. 1281–1358) from the circle of the "four Great Physicians of the time of the Chin and Yüan dynasties." Their biographies repeatedly identify them as far superior to the "common physicians" because they practiced medicine not as a profession, but merely now and then outside of their own family. Chang Ts'ung-cheng (A.D. 1156–1228) was another author from the circle of "the four great Chin and Yüan physicians," but he was known as an itinerant healer who practiced for his livelihood. When a disciple of Chang Ts'ung-cheng compiled his master's treatment experiences in a book he may for this same reason have chosen the title "How Confucian scholars can assist their relatives" (*Ju-men shih-ch'in*). We read, therefore, in an unsigned preface to the *Szu-k'u ch'üan-shu t'i-yao* edition of this work from the eighteenth century: "[Chang Ts'ung-cheng] has chosen the title *Ju-men shih-ch'in* because only Confucian scholars recognize the principles [of medicine] and because the person who wishes to assist his relatives has to possess some medical knowledge."[47]

The Categorization of Healers

Up to this point in the discussion on ethics several references to groups such as "Confucian physicians" (*ju-i*), "common physicians" (*yung-i*), and "enlightened physicians" (*ming-i*) have been made in the texts. These terms, which are clear value judgments, were never given an exact definition. Throughout the cen-

47. Chang Ts'ung-cheng, *Ju-men shih-ch'in*, in Wu Chung-hsi, *Yü-i shuang-pi*, ch. 8, p. 1.

turies the different groups which took part in the process of the distribution of the available medical resources in China developed numerous such designations in order to place themselves and other categories of healers in a comprehensive system.[48] Earlier we presented the text of Hsü Ch'un-fu (ca. A.D. 1556) (see above, pp. 40–41). Here we will cite a text by Li Ch'an (fl. A.D. 1575–80), the author of the *I-hsüeh ju-men*, an introductory work on medicine, as a second example of a comprehensive classification of all the healers recognized as physicians. It is interesting to note that Li Ch'an's listings include groups of healers who followed medical concepts which were considered heterodox by Confucian dogmatists. Li Ch'an selected 212 renowned persons from the history of medicine and grouped them, in an introductory chapter to his work, into the following five categories:

☐ Sages and exemplary persons of high antiquity [*shang-ku sheng-hsien*]. Wise rulers and exemplary ministers from the era of the three great ages and still earlier developed medicine and drugs to assist the dying as well as the living. [This is followed by eleven short biographies.]

Confucian physicians [*ju-i*]. From the time of the Ch'in and Han there existed [scholars] who mastered the classic authors and were extensively versed in history. They devoted themselves to the moral cultivation of the self and their way of life was marked by thoughtfulness. They are considered to be great Confucian scholars who also mastered medicine. [This is followed by 139 short biographies.]

Physicians practicing within a family tradition [*shih-i*]. They practice medicine as a profession and their knowledge is handed on over generations [within the family]. [This is followed by twenty-six short biographies.]

Virtuous physicians [*te-i*]. These are enlightened physicians [*ming-i*] or physicians practicing within a family tradition [*shih-i*] who have displayed their virtue. [This is followed by seventeen short biographies.]

Hermits in the mountains, Buddhists, and Taoists. [This is followed by nineteen short biographies.][49]☐

48. Up to now I have been able to confirm more than thirty terms of classification, not including the titles of medical officials.

49. Li Ch'an, *I-hsüeh ju-men*, introductory chapter, pp. 54a, 54b, 74a, 76a, 79a.

According to this wording "virtuous physicians" can be found both among the previously not clearly defined "enlightened physicians," and among the "physicians practicing within a family tradition." Consequently it remains uncertain whether in the author's point of view all Confucian physicians display virtue a priori. Li Ch'an also included Sun Szu-miao among the group of Confucian physicians, regardless of a quotation by Chu Hsi (see above, p. 38) which he inserted into the former's short biography: "Sun Szu-miao was a renowned *chin-shih* graduate at the time of the T'ang. As he was versed in medicine, he was deferred into the lower grade of the technicians [*chi-liu*]. How deplorable!"[50]

The considerations which induced Li Ch'an to admit a person into the group of the *ju-i* are, therefore, not in every case the same as those which lie at the basis of the method of classification used in this study. Li Ch'an obviously considered the type of training, practice, reputation and the influence on posterity as independent variables in his classification. I proceed from the way a practice is conducted, from the educational and social class background and, above all, from the interest formulated in the ethics advocated by an individual, in order to classify the specific person among one of the three main groups which I have defined as participating in the struggle for the distribution of resources. According to these criteria Chu Hui-ming (ca. A.D. 1590), whose ideas on medical ethics will be quoted below, has to be rated as one of the group of practicing physicians trained by Confucians, although his personal record did not correspond to the usual pattern.

Further Statements from Confucian Physicians

As may be seen from the different prefaces to his work *Tou-chen ch'uan-hsin lu*, Chu Hui-ming traced his genealogy over fourteen generations to Chu Hsi. For centuries his ancestors had taken up the career of Confucian scholars, were successful and gained a good reputation. Therefore Chu Hui-ming also prepared for such a future. Yet according to the report of his biographer, Tsang Mao-chung (ca. A.D. 1590), he repeatedly got into conflicts with government officials. Thus he finally changed his plans and studied medicine.[51] According to the report by Chu Feng-hsiang, possibly a contemporary relative of the author, Chu

50. Ibid., p. 56a.
51. Tamba, Mototane, *Chung-kuo i-chi k'ao*, p. 1346.

Hui-ming rationalized his leaving the Confucian career with the insight "that the men of letters from the past were of no benefit in this world and that Confucianism was in this respect by far inferior to other teachings."[52] Thus it can be well understood that in the ethics set forth in his work Chu Hui-ming explicitly advocated Buddhist principles. In this respect Chang Kao (see above, p. 42) can be considered his direct predecessor. Nevertheless several references to Confucianism can be found in Chu Hui-ming's work. As such we can consider both the anonymous and slightly falsified quotation from Confucius (see below, pp. 62–63), and Mencius' (372–289 B.C.) statement on the inherent goodness of man (see below, p. 62), which Chu Hui-ming renders with insignificant modifications.

Chu Hui-ming may have held a marginal position among Confucian physicians, yet the ideology and its values expressed in his ethics were characteristic of this group. He devoted four continuous sections to the theme of ethics; they are presented here in their full length, with the exception of the essay "A warning not to practice medicine without understanding its principle [*li*] and without knowledge of its literature," which is sufficiently characterized by its title. Chu Hui-ming chiefly stressed the purpose of giving service in medical practice and clearly rejected any profit orientation in this activity. Obviously he had read the work of Chang Kao, because he repeated one of his examples in order to underline the supernatural system of reward and requital.

In hardly any other text is the protective function of the formulated ethics displayed as openly as here. In addition to this, Chu Hui-ming recommended prognosis, that is to say an early withdrawal from incurable patients, and gave further instructions always with the rationale of protecting the physician against reproaches. It is remarkable that he does not mention the well-being or the interest of the patients in a single word. In regard to the official esteem enjoyed by physicians who practiced regularly outside the family and for reward, the significant parable is one in which he suggests the fate desirable for those wanting in the necessary veneration for physicians.

Finally it should be pointed out that Chu Hui-ming is the only one of the authors cited here who deplored the secrecy of know-

52. Ibid., p. 1345.

ledge. He saw his own mission as one of "handing on his mind" [*ch'uan-hsin*], a notion which reappears in the title of his work. Thus his biographer, Tsang Mao-chung, cited him in his own words:

☐ I have summed up my experience in defining cases of sickness into theoretical principles and have put them into writing in the following, so that every man can gain a full understanding of medicine by a single look into [this book]. Wherever my feet cannot carry me personally, my mind is to establish itself![53] ☐

The three sections on ethics selected from Chu Hui-ming's work read as follows:

☐ *PHYSICIANS SHOULD PRESERVE HUMANENESS*

The teaching of medicine is the teaching of Buddha. Since in this world man is struck by grave diseases, does not rise any more and advances toward death, compassion and pity arise, as it were, of their own accord in his neighbor. The latter takes pains to serve as a ferryman [in the sea of troubles]; [his help] does not resemble that of brokers looking for profit. And besides, which man who has received his life between heaven and earth would not possess a compassionate disposition by his very nature? For instance, if someone has to witness a child running into the danger of falling into a deep ravine, the [very threat] of an injury to the latter will move the person to pity, even in the case of an enmity between them. How much more does this apply to someone who devotes his entire life only to the purpose [of helping others in need]!

Those who share my viewpoint should always be aware that there is no difference between the poor and the rich, once they have reached the crossroads between life and death. They should not work toward great profits, but direct their full attention to those who remain dependent [on others] and should render their greatest compassion to those who have no one else to whom they could turn. Such conduct leads to a record of the greatest rewards in another world.

GOOD CONDUCT BRINGS REWARDS

An exemplary man of former times has made the following statement: "A physician who concentrates on issues of life and death and is nevertheless not formed by persistence, cannot pass

53. Ibid., p. 1346.

for a true [physician]!'' The teaching of medicine is exceedingly noble and the principles of medicine are difficult and subtle. Whoever accepts to practice this profession, should under no circumstances be negligent in any way. It is of special importance to direct one's attention to the right and the lofty.

Other people are to be regarded as oneself and it is to be considered a physician's duty to assist his fellow humans. If such actions are directed toward gain, they testify to poor morals. If self-interest is at play, the principle of humaneness is violated. Defective conduct of this nature does not solely occur among physicians, yet heaven and earth do not allow it in any case. Indeed!

In antiquity it was said: ''There are no two kinds of drugs for the lofty and the common; the poor and the rich receive the same medicine.'' If men could instill this into their consciousness, the high heavens would certainly not be without gratitude. Yet there are [physicians] who do not study the principles in the literature, who speak deceptively and give voice to the unfamiliar, who are filled with envy and foster suspicion, who promote only their own interests and harm others. They exploit diseases and perilous situations and demand copious presents [from their patients]. They value material goods highly, yet life has little value to them. Instead of spreading the information, they keep secret the books with prescriptions which prove to be useful. Such people are sure to encounter misfortune to their own body in the near future, and they will have to suffer in the far future. For the heavenly teaching is splendidly manifest. Though [its manifestations] may sometimes elude our understanding, in the end no one will escape its law. The point is to preserve respect!

During all the time in which he practiced medicine Chang Yen-ming did not even accept money or fabrics as a gift in return. When someone asked him for medicine he always hoped it would definitely develop its effectiveness. One day a fire broke out in the city. The heat and the flames spread everywhere. Amidst the flames only his dwelling remained untouched. Later on his children and grandchildren led a life of plenty.

We can learn from this example that the heavenly teaching had plainly revealed its reward of a good life.

I have been profoundly impressed by this occurrence. I have always retained an attitude of respect. One day I treated a case in Huai-chu. At night, when I was sleeping, a spirit appeared to me in my dream and said to me: "You should return quickly!" I woke up and was seized with fear. I excused myself immediately and returned home. Again I had a dream. I went to Hsi-pien and there an old man pushed me into the water. When I woke up, I found myself in my room surrounded by a glow of fire. Flames leaped toward the sky and the screams of my neighbors shook the earth. Then I spoke in my prayer: "Ever since I have been practicing my profession, I have not once sought my self-interest, so that a person would have lost his life, and I have never been careless, so that I would have brought about a patient's death. How could the protection by another world be refused to me!" After this a single bucket of water extinguished the flames which rose from the wood, and the [fire] receded. Everyone said: "The fact that you were surrounded by fire and yet were saved from it is due to the protection by the heavenly spirits which has been granted to you, because you are guided by a physician's moral principles!" From then on I persistently increased my efforts toward genuine motivations in helping all creatures.

One year had passed and I had rented an apartment in a market street. There one night an old man appeared to me in a dream and said: "You will experience discomfort. In this way the Lord on High intends to ascertain that you are truly guided by the moral principles of a physician. You have to preserve your patience for ten days, then you will be redeemed." I woke up and found myself in a strange mood. I locked the door and did not leave the house. Once, however, I was urged by a neighbor to take part in a drinking festivity. Three of the guests present conducted themselves immorally and without any reverence. They spit into my face and made insulting remarks. I remembered the prediction in my dream and did not let them perceive any [reaction] on my part. All the others took me for a coward. But then fully unexpectedly, those people were stricken by an epidemic and died within six days! Just as we can resist [worldly] foes one day, misfortune [which comes from the supernatural] can also be avoided!

Subsequently I only increased my reverence. In the place where I lived there was another colleague who was also guided by the moral principles of a physician. One day fire approached as far as his house, only there it receded and was extinct. Thence it becomes apparent that those who display a good way of life are certainly provided for from on high with full happiness. Unfortunately heaven does not go as far as to condemn the evil per se; it is probably for this reason that we [still] meet [also those] who adopt evil ways.

A WARNING TO DETERMINE THE PROSPECT
FOR A GOOD OR A BAD CURE EARLY ENOUGH

When treating a disease the physician observes a patient's coloring, listens to his sounds, asks him for his eating and drinking habits, his likes and dislikes, and feels [the patient's] pulse. All this together enables him to decide whether there exist good or bad prospects [for the cure of the specific patient].

In antiquity for instance when Yüeh-jen [i.e., Pien Ch'io] restored the prince of K'uo from death to life, he said: "He will live again" and was able to raise him. Another example is furnished by the illness of the prince of Huan, which could not be cured by a hot iron, nor by acupuncture, nor even by means of the *huo-ch'i* preparations. [Pien Ch'io] foresaw then [the fatal ending of the case] and left.[54] Today as in antiquity there is the [fatal] *kao-huang* condition.[55] In past times the physician Huan was not able to bring about any relief. [He explained the situation to his patient and was copiously rewarded.] Today however physicians are afraid to tell an unpleasant fact to a patient. Their hope to win money urges them on to aim for a success in every single case. Truth seems to be ready on their tongue but, in view of the circumstances, in the end they do not dare to utter it. Then suddenly their struggle will be lost, and they will have to accept rebukes. Hence if the physician announces any unpleasant facts at the very beginning, there will be no need to experience shame. If however [the patients or their relatives] come with reproaches in the end [because they had not been informed at the very beginning], who else then carries the responsibility but the physician himself?

Roughly speaking we can discern four different incorrect ways of handling the situation:

First: [The physician] knows exactly that good signs indicate [a possible] cure, yet he erroneously says that the signs are bad. In

54. Compare with this the biography of Pien Ch'io in the *Shih-chi,* ch. 105; a translation can be found in Bridgman, "La médecine dans la Chine antique," pp. 17–24.

55. Allusion to an event told in the *Tso-chuan,* VIII, Duke Ch'eng; cf. Legge, *The Chinese Classics,* vol. 5, pp. 372–4.

this manner he excites the patient greatly and can expect substantial reward.

Second: [The physician] diagnoses that the prospects [for a cure] are bad, and he nevertheless asserts that a successful treatment lies in the realm of the possible. He then acts in the hope that a fortunate chance will bring about a success so that his reputation will increase.

Third: The abilities [of the physician] are "common" and his knowledge is inadequate. His actions are immoderate and narrow-minded and he is not able to recognize the doors and ways which lead to life or death in their true significance. He assigns a wrong sense to the alternatives of a good and bad prospect [for a cure]. His words are not marked by experience and people suffer from his mistakes.

Fourth: The patient is obstinate and does not submit to his fate; the man who treats him makes every effort to spoil [the patient]. Without being able to lead his efforts to strengthen and assure [the patient] of a [successful] end, the damage will be aggravated. A mild [ailment] will thus develop into a grave [disease] and if one was able to speak initially of good indications, they are in the end bad omens. Although this is not a question of the attending physician's fault, he nevertheless will not be able to avoid being met with reproaches.

At every encounter with a disease physicians have therefore first to reflect on the case very conscientiously, and then they have to decide whether [a cure] is possible or not. They should not engage in the four [previously named] deceitful practices, and thereby bring shame on themselves. They should raise their eyes to the very exemplary conduct of Ch'in Yüeh-jen [i.e., Pien Ch'io] and take the sweet and fragrant writings on the physician Huan as their example.

They should not plan for a success, nor hope for profit, and neither should they handle the alternatives of death or life as a game. How then could it still happen that good and bad prospects are turned into their contrary, that adequate and unsuitable [treatments] are confused, that one is deceived for but a moment and that there is no end to gloating laughter over other people's misfortune![56] ☐

56. Chu Hui-ming, *Tou-chen ch'uan-hsin lu,* ch. 16, pp. 1b–3b, 5a–5b, in Ch'eng Yung-p'ei, *Liu-li chai i-shu shih-chung.*

Wang K'en-t'ang (ca. A.D. 1600) also was among that group of Confucian physicians who opposed the "common physicians" on the one hand, and, within their own group, the Confucians on the other hand. During the title of reign *wan-li* (A.D. 1573–1619) he graduated as a *chin-shih,* and obtained an administrative position in Fukien. Once, before he graduated, during his mother's illness, Wang K'en-t'ang witnessed how the attending physicians discussed different opinions. He found this very "common" and henceforth he directed his whole effort to prescriptions and the study of pharmacy. Shortly thereafter he was able to cure his sister's illness. Through this cure he became known among his neighbors and was called in for diagnoses and treatments. His own house is said to have frequently been full of patients. For some time his father observed this development, but then was possessed by apprehension that his son would give up a civil service career in favor of medical practice. After a serious admonition, Wang K'en-t'ang turned again to his preparations for the examinations. Not until he had graduated and was established as a civil servant did he continue to pursue his medical interests. At the age of eighty he fell ill unexpectedly. All the physicians who were consulted arrived at the conclusion that this was probably a case of old age, and they treated him accordingly. In the end the famous physician Li Chung-tzu (died A.D. 1655) was called. He diagnosed correctly and the cure soon followed. To this Wang K'en-t'ang is said to have responded: "At present there are but two physicians in the world and these are you and I!"[57] The contempt for the mass of physicians which is expressed in these words also makes itself felt in the following lines, taken from a preface which Wang K'en-t'ang composed for his work *Shang-han chun-sheng.* It is remarkable that he presents medicine itself as a praiseworthy resource created by the sages in antiquity. His criticism is directed against the use of these resources by "mediocre physicians" (*chung-i*):

☐ Where there is life, there is also dying. This holds good for the entire world. Yet death is not only a consequence of old age, it is already caused by diseases. This too holds good for the entire world and most especially for mankind. Therefore the sages [of antiquity] showed mercy and created medicine and the medica-

57. *Chung-kuo i-hsüeh ta-tz'u-tien,* p. 647.

ments. Now once there were medicine and the drugs, the people in the country no longer died from diseases, but from medicine and the drugs. Thereafter the wise men said: "If in case of a disease someone does not take any drugs at all, the results still resemble the success of a treatment by a mediocre physician." This is indeed credible![58] ☐

A Shift in Emphasis:
Confucian and Common Physicians Compete for Patients

Kung Hsin, who lived at about the same time as Wang K'en-t'ang, belonged to the group of practicing Confucian physicians. For a time he was working as a civil servant in the imperial office of medicine *(t'ai-i yüan)*. Beyond this he is known as the author of several medical works. In the *Ku-chin t'u-shu chi-ch'eng* we find three sections of formulated ethics composed by him in which Kung Hsin's interest, which reflects that of his group, is expressed. Kung Hsin considered himself as part of a core group of "enlightened physicians" *(ming-i)*. Although this term coincides largely with *ju-i* [Confucian physicians] and is, like the term *ju-i,* in contrast to the term "common physician" *(yung-i)*, we may observe by this time that the group of *ming-i* does not differ greatly from the "great physicians" *(ta-i)* of Sun Szu-miao. Evidently the gap between elite physicians practicing outside the Confucian paradigm and others who may be counted as practicing Confucian physicians had been narrowed considerably. With regard to the statements made by Sun Szu-miao and earlier Confucian writers concerning remuneration, it is important to note that professionalization of physicians had progressed sufficiently that their ethics could include the admonishment of patients not to be frugal when there was a question of expense.

And yet another element is new. Kung Hsin distinguishes his group from that of "common physicians" by the fact that he discourages his colleagues from soliciting patients by emphasizing individual skills. Here again we encounter a very important element in the efforts directed at professionalization, and one which is still found in our present society.[59] Patient solicitation,

58. Wang K'en-t'ang, *Shang-han chun-sheng* (preface by Wang K'en-t'ang, p. 1a), in Wang K'en-t'ang, *Liu-k'o chun-sheng.*
59. The rigorous observance of the law against solicitation is still counted among the main tenets of medical ethics, for instance, in Germany and in Britain. While in the USA this rule still exists nominally, there are a great number of offences known in which the professional organization of physicians has not

through emphasis on individual skills by one member of the group, implies that he is better than at least some of his colleagues. This kind of patient solicitation is therefore injurious to the group as a whole, because the public's attention is drawn to differences in performance. Differences in performance in their turn cause a lack of trust, and thus lessen the readiness of the public to entrust the same tasks to every member of the group.

☐ *WARNING WORDS TO ENLIGHTENED PHYSICIANS*

The enlightened physicians [*ming-i*] of today cultivate humaneness and righteousness in their attitude. Their study is extensive and embraces all of the writings in their entirety. For this reason they are well versed in theoretical medicine and its practical use. They know *yin* and *yang,* and understand the macrocosmic phases [*yün*] and the types of climate [*ch'i*]. Among the drugs they distinguish warm and cool [radiations of temperature]; among the pulsations they distinguish interior and exterior ones. For a treatment they apply procedures which replenish [*pu*] [deficiencies] or reduce [*hsieh*] [symptoms of excess] and among the diseases they distinguish between the symptoms of deficiencies [*hsü*] and the symptoms of excess [*shih*]. They make up their prescriptions according to the diseases and their mixtures of drugs are aimed at the symptoms. They ponder over the best procedures, are [flexible] in their treatments and do not cling mechanically to any formulas. They do not give themselves airs about empty fame, for the only thing they are interested in is effective help. Therefore they do not speculate about their success and neither do they plan for their own profit. A patient's wealth or poverty is of no concern to them. On the contrary they prescribe drugs according to a formula which is valid for everyone. Thus they have the dying rise again and bring back life. Their mercy resembles the mercy displayed by heaven and earth. Enlightened physicians who act in this way will be remembered for their virtue in all eternity.

WARNING WORDS TO COMMON PHYSICIANS

Today's common physicians [*yung-i*] brag about the unusual and the strange. They do not study the classic writings, neither do

---

intervened. At present there is a heated debate within the profession as to whether the issue of patient solicitation by physicians should be considered "unethical" or "ethical." Besides other instances, this development , too, is an indication of the beginning of the deprofessionalization of American physicians. Cf. Jack D. Martin, "New Dilemma for doctors."

they understand the meaning of their words. They praise themselves into the forefront in order to deceive the world around them. They compete and hurry from door to door; they enter on their own account, without being invited. Where there is an occasion, they offer themselves with small presents and ask the patient for his wishes. Then they give themselves airs about their skills and distribute all kinds of flattery; the sick themselves, however, remain uncertain. Finally they begin a confused treatment without having searched for the origin of the disease. They do not distinguish between symptoms of deficiency or excess; [the alternative] between life or death does not cause them any fear. Thus they are impetuous and unrestrained at the same time. If a disease takes an unexpected turn for the worse, they disappear quickly and have no concern for the fate of the afflicted. Their expectations and plans are solely directed toward profit. Common physicians who act in this way are a cause for shame and should be shunned.

WARNING WORDS TO PATIENTS

Nowadays patients frequently cut down on expenses. They are not willing to summon a physician quickly, on the contrary they wait until they are cured by themselves. They do not ask for recognized experts, but hope for a comfortable way. Without consideration for the peculiarity of the disease, they submit to trivial meaningless attempts. Some even pray to spirits and demons! Thus they resemble a boat which glides carefree through the hoarfrost and is suddenly stuck in solid ice. Then however they ask for a good physician, that is to say once the disease gives cause for alarm. Even if there existed miraculous drugs, it would be difficult to heal them in this condition. Foolishly they do not become aware [of the situation]. Once they finally come for a treatment after a great delay, they can only be told that their fate is sealed and that no blessing can be expected any more.

Such foolishness can only be deplored. Patients who conduct themselves in this manner should change their incorrect demeanor.[60]□

Kung T'ing-hsien (fl. A.D. 1615), the son of Kung Hsin, followed his father in many respects. He wrote numerous works and from time to time was employed in the imperial office for

60. Ch'en Meng-lei et al., *Ku-chin t'u-shu chi-ch'eng*, "Po-wu hui-pien," "I-shu tien," ch. 538; "I-pu," ch. 465, p. 62.

medicine. At the end of his well-known work *Wan-ping hui-ch'un,* he added his notions of ethics. These he expressed in ten maxims directed to physicians and patients respectively. In addition his ideas on ethics were included in four essays given in the same work. Kung T'ing-hsien progressed one step further than his father. He implicitly took up the discrimination against "common physicians" when he recommended that patients choose "enlightened physicians." A term such as *yung-i* does not appear anymore as an alternative, yet in its stead there again emerges a support for the *ju-i* group:

□ *TEN MAXIMS FOR PHYSICIANS*

In the first place they should adopt a disposition of humaneness; this is a justified demand. They should make a very special effort to assist the people and to perform far-reaching good deeds.

Secondly they should master the Confucian teachings. Confucian medical doctors are a precious help at all times. Their principles are valuable and enlightening; all of literature is open to them for consultation.

Thirdly they should be versed in the details of the pulse. It is necessary that they discern "interior" [*li*] and "exterior" [*piao*]. If they but lower their fingers [on the pulse], everything will be clear to them. Thus they will be able to cure those who are gravely ill.

Fourthly they are to recognize the causes of diseases. They have to be ready to speak about life and death. Only physicians who attain this stage are experts in their field.

Fifthly they should know the types of climate [*ch'i*] and the macrocosmic phases [*yün*], so as to understand the succession of the seasons. Accordingly they have to perform operations of replenishing [deficiencies] and reducing [over-abundances in the organism] with drugs of warm or cool temperature radiation, and to differentiate the treatments suitable at the time.

Sixthly they should be familiar with the different types of transportation channels; their understanding of them is not to give rise to any errors. If they are equally informed on the palaces [*fu*] and the granaries [*tsang*] of the body, they embody Pien Ch'io in the present.

Seventhly they should know the peculiarities of drugs and compose their prescriptions corresponding to the individual diseases. If they do not distinguish between warm and cool [qualities of drugs] they may endanger life.

Eighthly they should be informed on the preparation of drugs. They have to be familiar with the intensity of the fire [for the boiling of drugs] and the degree of fineness [for the drugs which have to be cut], in order to know what is too much and what is too little, what is dangerous and what is harmless.

Ninthly they should not be jealous, neither should they let themselves be guided by other people's favor or disfavor. The principles of heaven are lucid, they make us quickly aware of our mistakes.

Tenthly they should not esteem profits too highly, but instead cultivate humaneness and righteousness. Although we distinguish between the poor and the rich, there is but one type of drugs.

TEN MAXIMS FOR PATIENTS

In the first place they are to choose "enlightened physicians" [*ming-i*] and thereby receive help in their ailment. They have to be careful, because life and death follow each other closely.

Secondly they should be willing to take remedies. With their help even a person who has already fallen ill can yet get rid of his ailment. There are many foolish people who hinder themselves [by not taking remedies].

Thirdly they should have the treatment started at an early stage. At the beginning it is still simple. Whoever fails to be careful in hoarfrost will suddenly be surprised by solid ice.

Fourthly they should not have sexual intercourse, then their sufferings will cease by themselves. If however they act contrary to this maxim, even a divine physician will be at his wits' end.

Fifthly they should guard against any excitement and should be very careful in this respect. If a person is angry, the flames flare up in him. This creates great difficulties in bringing help and in checking [the disease].

Sixthly they should beware of wrong thoughts and take care of themselves in peace. If they avoid all troubles, the mind will find peace by itself.

Seventhly they should eat and drink moderately. The preparation of food is to follow the rules. Too much is harmful to the mind; satiation is difficult to digest.

Eighthly they should be concerned about their getting up and their getting rest. They have to reduce their social life; even slightly increased stress will drain the vitality.

Ninthly they should not believe in the heterodoxical [in medicine]. Such a belief is harmful. Alien principles are misleading; they deceive the people and make them uncertain.

Tenthly they should not fear expenses. What sense is there in economizing here! I ask you, what is more precious, life or material goods?[61]

When someone falls ill in the south and a physician is called for the diagnosis, he is merely asked for a prescription and someone is sent to buy the drugs in the market. The people are not concerned as to whether the particular drugs are genuine or falsified, whether they have been properly prepared, and finally whether they are taken as prescribed. If there is no effect, they do not blame it on their own omissions, but speak of the physician's "commonness" [*yung*]. The next day they confide in yet another physician. This is repeated several times and the illness only gets worse. Naturally the physicians are also misled and confused and cannot account for the reasons of the prolonged process [of the cure]. Unquestionably the causes are to be sought in the patient's failure to comply and in the fact that the physicians are not enlightened.

When someone in the north is taken ill, and a physician is called into the house, the seriousness of the disease will not be discussed with him. He is given one or two pieces of gold and asked for one or two prepared drugs which are then to show immediate results. If they do not act, the [patients] turn to other physicians. In the morning they turn to Ch'in and in the evening they turn to Ch'u! The people are not aware that the human constitution goes through states of deficiencies and symptoms of excess and that the diseases themselves can occur in a superficial or an aggravated form. Now one or two preparations of drugs for a cold or an ailment which appears between the skin and the flesh may well be sufficient for a cure, yet this is certainly not the case with diseases based on inner damages or painful ailments and consumption! Yet this bad habit is widespread among the people. Only those who know are able to distinguish.

61. Kung T'ing-hsien, *Wan-ping hui-ch'un*, ch. 8, pp. 34a–34b.

In former times the principles of medicine were called "principles of the hermits in the mountains" [*hsien-tao*], and originally they were applied with the aim of keeping men alive. Yet in many cases physicians nowadays do not know this old significance. When they visit the rich, they are conscientious; when they deal with the poor, they act carelessly. This is the eternal peculiarity of those who practice medicine as a profession, and not as applied humaneness! According to my opinion medicine means responsibility over life and death, and this cannot be taken lightly. How could I be generous on one occasion and petty on the other, just because some are rich and the others are poor? To those who agree with me I say that they should adopt the virtue of the highest as their own attitude, which consists of love of life. We should not divide the poor and the rich; likewise they are all living people! This too is a hidden merit which the powers of another world will register.

When they call a physician for help we frequently observe nowadays that people have the patient lie in a dark room within an area concealed by fabrics. They do not inform the physician what the suffering consists of and merely allow him to feel the pulse. As to women, he is frequently not allowed to see them at all. How can he pass judgment on the patient's voice and appearance under such circumstances? Moreover they cover the patient's hand with a fine brocade, and they dislike it if the physician poses questions. But if they allow him to pose questions, he does not receive any answer. In this manner they can certainly not wish any cure for their disease; the physician will have the greatest difficulties.

Probably the people do not know that the divine physicians of days gone by made use of the four diagnostic procedures of looking, hearing and smelling, questioning, and feeling the pulse. If only one of these four is left out, the disease will not be recognized. Moreover today's physicians are hardly comparable to the divine physicians of antiquity. How then should they, especially they, diagnose the condition of those parts of the organism which are responsible for collecting and storing [influences from the outside] merely by feeling the pulse? I write this down here, in order to alert those who suffer from a disease to the fact that if they call a physician, they [should] inform him of everything pertaining to the ailment, as well as let him inspect the symptoms personally and feel the pulse, until he has understood everything and every doubt has been removed. In the past [Su] Tung-p'o [A.D. 1036–1101] said: "I am solely concerned about healing diseases; how could medicine become an end in itself for me?"

Among my colleagues there are some practitioners with a bad character. They have specialized in praising themselves for their excellence and in revealing the drawbacks of others.

Whenever they come to a patient, they do not ask after his ailment, but solely criticize the mistakes of the physician who has treated him before, in order to instill fear and apprehension in patients. Now if the medicaments of the physician who gave the preliminary treatment were fully justified, why should we look for others? Supposing that due to an imbalance on one occasion the treatment still has not led to any results, how is it possible to ascribe the use of the earlier drugs to the "commonness" [of the physician who had given the preliminary treatment]? In the long run, medicine is based on the principles of humaneness. Moreover we are basically a community of colleagues due to the handing down [of our knowledge] by way of teacher-student relationships. Even if there are insignificant discrepancies, we nevertheless have to protect each other and on no account are we to expose one another! We should thereby of course not lose our highly principled ways of life. Caution! Caution![62]□

Before turning to two other contemporary voices from the group of practicing Confucians, I wish to cite a later author who conveys how little Kung T'ing-hsien's ethics convinced the more rigid Confucian physicians. Lin Ch'i-lung, a civil servant who graduated as a *chin-shih* during the rule of *shun-chih* (A.D. 1644–61), but later on lost his position as a civil servant, wrote in the year 1666:

□ There are numerous people who practice medicine, yet there are only a few who study medicine. With self-assurance they advance theories and they write books thoughtlessly. Summaries of the available material are handed on from one to the other. What is genuine is thereby lost, and it is the fault of those who teach such medicine. What a shame! Especially now, since the

62. Ibid., pp. 34b–35b.

Wan-ping hui-ch'un and other books by Mr. Kung T'ing-hsien have been circulated far and wide, there is no medicine at all left in the country. His readers open one book cover in the morning and the very evening they dare to examine diseases and make prescriptions. To them medicine is not the "practice of humaneness," to help in need and to support in danger, but a comfortable way by means of which they rapidly obtain clothes and food. They consider medicine as something superficial! They consider medicine as something to be taken lightly! How then can there still be renowned physicians in the country![63]□

Ch'en Shih-kung's (fl. A.D. 1605) ethics agrees largely with the tendency, apparent in the earlier statements by the group of practicing Confucians, to raise the value of medical practice. According to his explanations, he appears to belong to the group around Kung Hsin and Kung T'ing-hsien, that is to those physicians who practice for profit but who nevertheless number themselves in the class of Confucian physicians. If we compare Ch'en Shih-kung's ethics with earlier statements we have read, one observes that it contains several new dimensions. For example he gives advice on how a physician may gain access to such risky patients as prostitutes, and furnishes perhaps the first advice on capital investment for physicians who have accumulated great earnings. The group consciousness is expressed as clearly as with Kung T'ing-hsien; not only does Ch'en Shih-kung advise against criticizing one's colleagues in front of patients, he recommends conduct within the group which we might describe as "friendly." From here to the organization of a professional group is but a small step.

Ch'en Shih-kung does not continue the discrimination between an elite core group and "second rate" physicians; he speaks only of physicians. For the first time we read concrete statements calling for the prohibition of advertising, and we especially note the author's urging of a continuing education for physicians. Ch'en Shih-kung expressed himself in particular as follows:

□ *FIVE ADMONITIONS TO PHYSICIANS*

Firstly. When called to a patient, the physician is to go there immediately, regardless of whether it is a question of high-ranking

---

63. Chai Liang, *I-hsüeh ch'i-meng hui-pien*, preface by Lin Ch'i-lung, pp. 1b–2b.

or low-ranking people, poor ones or rich ones. He is not to postpone [the doctor's visit] or even decline it. He is not to give the
impression that he has the intention of coming if he will not come
after all; this would be interpreted as unfriendliness. Regardless of
whether the money received for drugs amounts to much or little,
or whether the physician receives anything at all, he is always to
act with his whole heart and according to a single guiding principle. In this manner day by day the business will increase by itself
and his conscience will nevertheless not be affected.

Secondly. When making a visit to a sick married woman,
widow or a nun, the physician has to have a companion. Only
then can he enter the room [of the particular person] and undertake
the examination. If the disease is of a very private nature, he has
to preserve a great integrity more than ever. Not even in the
presence of his own wife is he allowed to speak of such cases. The
reason for this command lies in the seclusion of the rooms for
women.

Thirdly. The physician is not allowed to take home pearls,
amber or other precious things from his patients, under the pretext
of using them for medication, while in reality to keep them for
himself and replace them with worthless objects. Wherever the
use of such materials seems necessary, the patients themselves
should be asked to undertake the preparation. If, then, after having taken them, recovery does not set in, no suspicion falls upon
the physician. Besides the value of other people's possessions
should never become a target. Such a mode of conduct does not
befit a noble man.

Fourthly. Whoever holds a medical practice is not to give
himself to any pleasure or to mountain climbing, wine and the
fondness for travel. He is not to leave his practice, even for a very
short moment. Whenever a patient arrives, he has to be examined
personally and his medicaments have to be prepared with care. In
their composition the recipes have to agree with the formulas of
the classics for prescriptions, and their parts have to be listed on a
label. A limitation of the prescription would call forth opposition
[from the patients].

Fifthly. If asked for an examination by prostitutes or their
escorts, they should be treated like the daughters of free families.
Those who have second thoughts or conduct themselves childishly
only harm their own reputation. Once an examination is con-

cluded, the physician should return home immediately. Only when the ailment subsides is it legitimate to send drugs [to the specific patients as an after-treatment]. On no account is one to go there once more in the hope of an obscene reward.

TEN MAXIMS FOR PHYSICIANS

Firstly. Above all they are to know the principles of Confucianism, only then will they be able to understand the practice of medicine. Regardless of whether they turn to inner or outer medicine, they have to study conscientiously the books which contain the genuine insights of the enlightened physicians of antiquity. The writings are not to leave their hands either by day or by night; they have to consult every single work and get to know it. They are to collect the diverse aspects of literature and to remember it mentally and visually. Whenever they are then faced with a disease, they will quite automatically avoid making mistakes.

Secondly. At the choice and the purchase of medicinal drugs they should follow Lei-kung's[64] formulas for their prescription. They are to prepare the drugs in accordance with the formulas for prescriptions and compound them and increase or reduce them in conformity with the individual disease and the respective seasons. Decoctions and powders are to be prepared freshly. Pills and preparations of chemical drugs [*tan*] should be kept in stock. Plasters will be more effective the longer they lie in store; similarly the effectiveness of drug-releasing tampons [*mien-yao*] increases with time. With drugs there is no economizing with the costly; in the end it will be worth it.

Thirdly. Colleagues from the vicinity should not be offended thoughtlessly or treated without respect. When associating with such persons one should be friendly and cautious. Older people should be respected, educated people should be regarded as teachers; conceited colleagues should be avoided, and to those who are not as advanced as oneself one should offer one's help. In this way slander and hatred stay away on their own account, and trust and harmony will be esteemed highly.

Fourthly. The managing of a household resembles the treatment of a disease. When a person does not take care of his vital forces, but wastes them in excess, various ailments will arise. In mild cases the body loses its members; in severe cases life itself is

---

64. Legendary ancestor of the traditional pharmaceutical technology in China.

destroyed. When the management of a household is not moderate, but extravagantly luxurious and wasteful, day after day there will be [financial] imbalance. In mild cases the reserves will then be missing, in grave cases want and misery will develop.

Fifthly. Man receives his destiny from heaven: he is not to bear any ill will against heavenly fate. If he is looking for a profit, he has to account for himself whether this intention can be reconciled with his conscience or whether it violates the principles of heaven. That which agrees with the principles of heaven strengthens the interpersonal relationship. Yet that which is contrary to them brings misfortune which will extend to the children and grandchildren. Therefore why should not men attach little value to profit and keep harm at a distance, in order to avoid the misfortune of a later requital?

Sixthly. When [physicians] wish to express their feelings toward their relatives and friends in their own dwelling place, presents should not be conspicuous or unusual in any way, with the exception of congratulations for weddings and of consolations for cases of death or sickness. When [physicians] give a banquet, it is to consist only of a course of fish and a course of vegetables. For one this reduces the expense and saves on salary. For it is said: "Conscientiousness and frugality surpass far-reaching presumption!"

Seventhly. [Physicians] are not to take money for drugs from the poor or those in distress, from travelling beggar priests, be they Buddhists or Taoists, nor from messengers of the local administration who come for treatment. It is befitting to provide these people with drugs free of charge. Even if a person is in need and has difficulties in another respect, he should be given something, as far as this lies in one's power. Such conduct is applied humaneness. Otherwise it can happen that a person has the medicaments, but neither fire nor food. His life would nevertheless be endangered.

Eighthly. Savings, regardless of whether it is a matter of little or much, should be invested in real estate. In this way one creates a basis. [Physicians] should not waste their possessions on pleasures or objects of luxury. It is also inappropriate for them to frequent gambling establishments or wine houses; this would only harm their business. In such things they have to restrain themselves rigidly. Only thus can slander and hatred be avoided.

Ninthly. All medicinal drugs and utensils which [physicians] keep in their practice should be prepared conscientiously and remain in a flawless condition. In case of an emergency, it will not do that anything is missing. To perfect their personal knowledge [physicians] have thoroughly to study old and new books of former sages and present-day publications of medical works by known authors. This is evidently a basic duty for all physicians.

Tenthly. If a physician receives a call from an administrative official, he has to respond to this promptly and should not be negligent. He has to meet these people with sincere respect, explain to them the cause of their illness and give them a prescription. Once the disease has been cured, he is not to hope for a testimonial plaque or a present on any account. Neither is he [to exploit such a relationship] to stand up for someone else and thus commit a violation. Outside of such professional occasions, physicians should not frequent civil servants; they have to make it their duty to keep the laws.[65]□

About one and a half centuries later, Hsü Ta-ch'un (A.D. 1693–1771), a notable medical author, published a new edition of the *Wai-k'o cheng-tsung* by Ch'en Shih-kung. He made minor changes in the wording of the second admonition:

□ Secondly. When making a visit to a sick married woman, widow, or a nun, a companion is indispensable. Only then may the physician enter the room [of the person in question] and carry out the examination. If now suddenly the companion is not present anymore, everything imaginable has to be done to avoid suspicion, and to carry out the examination with the greatest integrity. It is not permitted to speak unguardedly about the [intimacies of other] boudoirs even with one's own wife.[66]□

Evidently Hsü Ta-ch'un had the opinion that in the meantime physicians had come into such great public trust that they were able to visit particular female patients even without a companion, provided all the rules of conduct were preserved; this would show a considerable step forward in professionalization. Yet in his wording there exist undertones implying that the situation described is a possible trap. It was still advisable to exercise special caution.

65. Ch'en Shih-kung, *Wai-k'o cheng-tsung*, ch. 8, pp. 125–128, in Li T'ao, "Chung-kuo ti i-hsüeh tao-te-kuan," pp. 271–3.
66. Ch'en Shih-kung, *Wai-k'o cheng-tsung*, revised edition by Hsü Ta-ch'un, ch. 12, pp. 22a–22b.

The explanations of the two Kung and of Ch'en Shih-kung may give the impression that the group of Confucians practicing medicine had already detached itself so far from their mother group and drawn nearer to the independent physicians, and that this had led to formation of a large group of physicians tolerated by Confucianism. Such an impression would, however, be erroneous. The statements by Chang Chieh-pin (fl. A.D. 1624) and by Chang Lu (A.D. 1627–1707) demonstrate that the process was still not completed in the seventeenth century.

Chang Chieh-pin was the son of a favorite at the court of a prince and came to the nation's capital at the age of fourteen. At first he had explored a military career. As his expectations did not come about, he joined the independently practicing physician Chin Meng-shih and studied medicine with him. He made a name for himself as an advocate of the teachings of Li Kao (see above, p. 58) and of Hsüeh Chi (fl. A.D. 1530), whom he frequently quoted in his writings. Both Li Kao and Hsüeh Chi were Confucian physicians. Hsüeh Chi was employed for a long time as an imperial medical official and a court physician.

Chang Chieh-pin's close attachment to the group of independently practicing physicians and his simultaneous efforts to continue a tradition of medical concepts developed by Confucian physicians make it possible for us to understand the formulated ethics which he put down under the title "Record [of an instruction] that medicine is not a petty teaching [*hsiao-tao*]." Chu Hsi's judgment concerning medicine does not seem to have lost in emphasis in the least and was enforced by orthodox Confucianism. Chang Chieh-pin's ethics was directed at this group and is based on the teachings of the Sung neo-Confucians. His ethical statements are far more skillful in linking professional medicine with the values and the theoretical argumentation of its "opponents" than is the case in other texts with a similar intention. In addition Chang Chieh-pin is the only author with a formulated ethics who does not assert his statements directly, but uses the stylistic technique of impersonal presentation by putting his arguments into the mouth of a "strange man" from the wilderness:

☐ *RECORD [OF AN INSTRUCTION] THAT MEDICINE*
   IS NOT A PETTY TEACHING

When I was already advanced in years I undertook a journey into the wilderness of the eastern border regions. There I met a strange person who looked at me casually and then asked me: "Did you also study medicine? Medicine is difficult; it demands the greatest conscientiousness from you!" Whereupon I replied: "Although medicine is a petty teaching, its concern focuses on life. How could I dare not to be aware of [the necessity for] conscientiousness. I take note of your instructions with respect." The stranger became very angry and addressed me in a voice filled with disdain: "In any case you do not belong to those who are familiar with medicine! If you claimed just now of your own accord that the aim of medicine is life, how can you say then at the same time that this is a matter of a petty teaching? The principle [*tao*] of life has its origin in the principle of the universe [*t'ai-chi*] and is distributed over the entirety of all things. Not until life sprang forth did the five social relationships develop. Therefore creation constitutes, as it were, the forge of life, and the teaching of the principle [*tao-hsüeh*] is considered the guiding principle of life, and medicine and the drugs are the nurses of life. Thence it becomes evident that the significance of medicine is deeply rooted and that its assertions encompass a wide scope. Only superhuman intelligence has the power to advance to its most subtle details, and only the enlightenment to adhere to the middle position suffices to discern even the last details. An understanding of the basic traits and details of the medical principles corresponds to [an understanding of] the principles of peaceful government. An understanding of the effect and the failure of the medical principles corresponds to [an understanding of] the momentum of rise and decline. An understanding of the hesitation and of the urgency of the medical principles corresponds to [an understanding of] the mechanisms of attack and defense. An understanding of the change and the persistence of the medical principles corresponds to [an understanding of] the significance of social intercourse and private life. Whoever is penetrated inwardly by the principles [*li*] and the influences [*ch'i*] can point to the changes and transformations [of all things] and calculate them. Whoever is in command of the connections of *yin* and *yang* to the point where he can play with them 'on the palm of his hand,' for him the walls of separation and the outside walls do not represent an obstacle to perceive [all things].

"Through the discipline of his body and his mind the Confucian scholar treats himself to complete honesty [*ch'eng-shih*]. The

Buddhist and the Taoist treat themselves by purging themselves of faults in their previous lives through perfect observance of moral rules and [a life of] sincerity. Body and mind of other people and of oneself are unified by the principle [*li*]. Hence whoever perceives that which is close by, perceives also that which is distant; whoever understands well that which is distant, also understands well that which is close at hand. Therefore it is said: 'If there are truthful [*chih*] people, there is true knowledge; if there is true knowledge, there is also a true medicine.' How is it therefore possible to say that medicine is trivial?

"But wherever we turn we find superficiality and commonness. [A patient's] itching is eliminated by pepper and sulphur, onions and shallots relieve [a patient] of his winds. Has anyone ever said: 'This is not medicine'? If someone but wears a black coat or a yellow cap, he is immediately called a Buddhist or a Taoist priest. And if someone speaks in an affected manner and displays pretentious mannerisms, what else could he be [in the eyes of the people] but a Confucian! Yet not even in the course of the same day would one speak of the mountains of *t'ai-shan* and of some small hills, of the streams and the sea and some ditches of water.

"Whoever has no understanding of *yin* and *yang,* and meddles with symptoms of excess and conditions of deficiency without knowing about them, whoever is endowed with a careless mind and the nature of a daredevil, hides in a cave and is one-sided and 'common,' will certainly not only fail to accomplish anything good, but on the very contrary he will cause harm [wherever he practices]. Such people do not even reach the level of those who use pepper, sulphur, onions and shallots, not to mention that they deserve the designation 'petty teaching' [for their activity]. On what basis would one be able to talk to them at all about medicine?

"Medicine is certainly difficult! Medicine is certainly sublime! It represents the earliest tradition of genuine supernatural and exemplary people, and the first duty of a people.

"My son you should not belittle it because it is apparently but a matter of herbs and trees. You should endeavor to penetrate to the realm where essence [*ching*] and spirit [*shen*] are joined, and proceed to the border regions, where the dark meets the mysterious. Once you understand the beginning and the end of all processes, and once you have grasped the origin and consequences of a result, it can be said that you have accomplished something in this field [of medicine]. You certainly have to take the greatest pains!''

I listened to this instruction and was profoundly disconcerted and greatly alarmed. I muttered some words in exchange and withdrew. My agitation lasted for several months. So as not to forget these admonitions, I have put them down here in writing.[67]□

Before turning to Chang Lu and his arguments, I intend to point out one more aspect of the continuing process of professionalization of expert physicians as it becomes obvious in a preface by Lu Ch'i (A.D 1614–?) to the *Che-kung man-lu,* a work by Huang Ch'eng-hao, which had been written approximately in 1636. Huang Ch'eng-hao was a *chin-shih* graduate of the time of *wan-li* (A.D. 1573–1619). He held a civil service position in Fukien and studied medicine because he himself had always been weak and sickly. Lu Ch'i's biographers relate that he had become a Buddhist priest after the suicide of one of his brothers and after a time of seclusion. Due to pressure from his mother, he apparently gave up this status, and in the end he returned to his house. Lu Ch'i is said to have had special ability in the field of medicine, which he applied in the care of his relatives. Yet he is said to have helped outside the family when asked to do so. This he frequently did without charging anything. This type of medical practice corresponded fully to the Confucian ideal. Lu Ch'i's explanations suggest that this practice did not always enjoy the highest reputation with the population, who evidently preferred the experts despised by the Confucians.

□ Whoever is in need of a physician nowadays either chooses an old man who is already losing his teeth, or one of the honorable figures who ''ride along on blue birds and are splendidly clothed.'' The clothing [of these people] is elegant and their name plaques are kept in thickly printed letters. They are generally called ''renowned physicians'' [*ming-i*]. Others give themselves airs about traditions handed down over many generations and boast of secret recipes. Yet their ability to read does not suffice even to discern a six from a seven and they do not know how to spell the names of the simplest drugs. Still the patients invite such

67. Chang Chieh-pin, *Chang-shih Ching-yo ch'üan-shu,* ch. 3, p. 22b.

practitioners with respect and refer to them as "physicians with expertise" [*chuan-i*]. Well, yes!

If Confucian scholars are not able to apply [their knowledge] exhaustively to the problems of the world in the civil service, this possibility remains open to them only in the field of medicine. For such an activity they are especially suited! Yet if someone declares [in the presence of a patient to whose care he intends to contribute]: "I am a Confucian scholar," the people who are already discussing the treatment of the particular case will quite inevitably spit in his face. Well, yes! Does heaven not reject those here who desire to find support [in medicine] as their aim in life? And is this not a difficult theme to discuss with simple people?[68]□

Orthodox Confucianism Criticizes the Degree of
Professionalization Reached by Practitioners

In 1695 Chang Lu (A.D. 1627–1707) wrote a remarkable ethics, which contains the most vehement attacks against professional physicians from the point of view of orthodox Confucianism. It is not certain whether Chang Lu himself had ever passed the Confucian examinations. His biographers only mention that he concentrated on Confucian learning from his youth to prepare for a suitable career. Yet the fall of the Ming dynasty, which Chang witnessed approximately in his twenties, thwarted all such plans. Possibly due to his loyalty to the Ming, he retreated for more than ten years to a remote mountain range. Later on he returned to the medical science in which he had shown an especial interest ever since his youth, and became known as the editor and publisher of several medical studies.

Chang Lu couched his ethics in "ten warnings to physicians." He also avoided the differentiation into distinct groups of physicians by means of the discriminating terms previously in use. He speaks only of the "masters of the prescriptions" [*fang-chia*] and uses a term which we have so far encountered only in the modification *fang-chi* (see above, p. 37).

As someone who was pledged to Confucianism, Chang Lu could not tolerate the fact that new "primary" resources had been introduced into medicine and that these stood outside of the Con-

68. Huang Ch'eng-hao, *Che-kung man-lu,* preface by Lu Ch'i, pp. 1a–1b, in Ch'eng Yung-p'ei, *Liu-li chai i-shu shih-chung.*

fucian comprehensive paradigm. He tried to ridicule such tendencies by examples from biographies in the *Shih-chi* on Pien Ch'io and Ts'ang-kung Shun-yü I. The latter refer back almost 2000 years.[69]

Chang Lu is the only author of a formulated ethics who insists on different treatment for rich and poor. The opinion which is admitted quite openly in the fourth warning, that a physician of the ideal type is not to respond to every call, likewise corresponds to this maxim, which aims at a preservation of the social stratification. A further element which Chang Lu considered worth emphasizing was the use of prognosis to withdraw from hopeless cases. Both this statement and the recommendation not to respond to every call imply a renunciation of "secondary" resources.

Chang Lu's ethics may be considered as an expression of the endeavor to revoke the professionalization of the Confucian physicians which in some ways had progressed too far. Chang Lu did not pursue this effort very far, and maybe it was not possible any more to do so. The receipt of money, with the exception of those patients who neither want to nor are able to pay, does not present any conflict of conscience to him. A sense of group cohesion which prohibits criticism among colleagues is also strongly marked in his work:

☐ *TEN WARNINGS OF SHIH-WAN LAO-JEN*
    TO THE PHYSICIANS

[*First*] *warning: Model practice and deplorable practice*—
Teachers who do not look as if they were crouching on benches, geomancers who do not speak unceasingly about their field of study, Buddhist priests who do not wield their scepter everywhere, alchemists who do not show their cinnabar and, finally, physicians who do not demonstrate their ability to prescribe recipes at every occasion, all these resemble great painters who express themselves by a few strokes of their paint brush. They are the true masters!

It is a different matter with those physicians who belong to the clique of those going about with a bag filled with drugs. If they did not let themselves be heard everywhere, there would remain

69. Cf. note 54; in addition Bridgman, "La médecine dans la Chine antique," pp. 24–50, offers a translation of the biography of Ts'ang-kung Shun-yü I from the *Shih-chi*, ch. 105.

nothing for them which could secure them a great name. If they did not frequent the lowest civil servants, there would be no opportunity for them to enter the houses of those who belong to the administration. If they did not continuously carry their opinion on their tongue, they would be incapable of reaching the highest gain. If they did not open their doors to the carts and horses of others, they would not have any opportunity to win admiration from their neighbors. Finally, if they did not embellish their practices with flags of gratitude and plaques of acknowledgments, they would not have anything else to prove their ability anew daily. Yet, if not exercised with supernatural perfection, even these five [deplorable] manners of conduct are not suitable for anyone to reach [success] in medicine as if he had found a shortcut. Only those scholars who are true to the principles and unselfish, who cannot adapt themselves to common customs and who remain at a distance from the fashionable, follow the natural course of events.

[*Second*] *warning: Incorrect behavior relying on one's special skills*—Those who devoted their entire attention to medicine were counted for ages either among the sages and exemplary persons, scholars and professors, or at least among the celestial and sublime hermits. Nevertheless, none attained access to the dynastic histories. The great historiographer [Szu-ma Ch'ien, 145–80 B.C.] has chosen [from this group of persons] the very Pien Ch'io and Ts'ang-kung and included them in the biographies [of his work on history]. This certainly did not happen without a special purpose in mind. In doing this he expressed the opinion that Pien Ch'io, who adapted himself in his practice to the fashion of his time, encountered misfortune because [of the public exhibition] of his abilities, and that Ts'ang-kung, who hid himself from the public and lived in seclusion, was slandered because he did not agree with the conditions of his time. Is there not the specific mistake expressed here that a person relying on his special abilities engages in wrong conduct? How much more does this apply to those [physicians] who do not possess the abilities of a Pien Ch'io or a Ts'ang-kung, and who nevertheless give themselves airs about the extraordinary! Why do they not acknowledge the documented events of the past as exemplary [for their own situation]?

[*Third*] *warning: Obstinacy and one-sidedness*—Men suffer from the fact that they consider drugs to be unimportant, and physicians suffer from their own one-sidedness. [The first of these two points] is based on the fact that many people are not aware of how important [drugs] can be for them which are completely unknown to them, and that they do not acquiesce calmly in what is prescribed to them.

The responsibility of physicians consists in supplementing one-sidedness and in aiding in misfortune. Therefore they use very special drugs with a marked one-sided effectiveness, so as to regulate extreme one-sided influences.

In the past all those who have gained a name for themselves, were exclusively guided by their own opinions, which could differ as much as ice and fire. Recklessly they tried out whatever struck them suddenly. In this way one-sidedness became harmful and the principles lost their balance.

I wish everyone in this wide world would observe the following warning with all his heart: "If someone is sick and does not treat this disease at all, he will usually obtain the same results which a treatment from a mediocre physician would have given." Now if a physician [is not even mediocre, but] possesses only one-sided skills, who then should offer a chance to such a [practitioner] to apply his art?

[*Fourth*] *warning: Wrong acquaintances spoil one's character*—Physicians highly value the tendencies of a time and look down upon the traditional. Therefore, there is no difference [in what regards chance] between a game of cards and [the moments in which] their hands are capable of carrying out that which their mind envisions.

Those who are good chess players are called "experts" [*kuo-shou*]. The same designation "experts" also exists for physicians. Basically chess is founded on the principles of attack and defense. And the loss of but one single piece influences all the schemes of the game. Physicians hold power over security and danger [for the life of their patients] in their hands. The erroneous application of but one drug has an effect on the life or death [of the treated patient]. Now if [as a physician] one associates day in and day out with one's contemporaries and makes it one's task to be the single outstanding one among them, one will not fare differently than the champion in chess who participates everywhere in every game.

Though the prize be certainly his, his mind and his hands will weaken by the day. His thoughts will become superficial and lose their depth; his character will be confused and common. What reason is there then to continue to follow such a mediocre person?

[*Fifth*] *warning: To miss reality, because of the name given*—When a medical doctor visits a patient, he has to diagnose and name the latter's disease and to compare treatments. In this manner he avoids misleading himself or his fellow-men. Today's masters of the prescriptions [*fang-chia*] act differently.

As soon as they diagnose a "development of heat" [*fa-je*], they classify it as "injury caused by the cold" [*shang-han*]. Without specifying in any way, they then set up restrictions in regard to eating and drinking and make use of the entire scale of "dispersing" [*fa-san*] and "draining" [*hsiao-tao*] drugs. Just how could they know that among the diseases caused by the cold only two symptoms require restrictions in food, and these are the injury of the constructive influences [*ying*] through the cold and the injury of both the constructive and the protective influences [*wei*]? If, for example, it is, on the contrary, a matter of an injury of only the protective influence through wind, then there is no rule which prescribes restrictions in regard to eating. On the contrary, it is said that [in such a case] a hot pulp is to be swallowed to reinforce the effect of the medicine.

A damage of the constructive influences caused by the cold which becomes apparent in the pulse only after a time, or which is accompanied by intolerable sudden perspiration, can be slightly strengthened internally and balanced externally by the use of the sweetness of gelatin sugar or wheat in decoction of cinnamon. This success is based on the method of inducing changes by a hot pulp, which belongs to the experiences of a beginner in the treatment of the *t'ai-yang* diseases. Even in severe winters one rarely encounters anyone who makes the effort to specify the afflicted transportation channels and to distinguish between different methods of treatment in the case of actual damage through the cold.

The schools of thought of recent times superficially diagnose the most diverse diseases as "damages, through cold, related to the four seasons" [*szu-shih shang-han*]. They do not discern between temporarily weakened influences [*fu-ch'i*] and others which [are intensified] due to the seasons [*shih-ch'i*]. In indiscriminately treating every case of this nature with drugs which are advisable for diseases caused by wind, they kindle as it were the fire in the stove still more. And if there is indeed internal damage linked to a deficiency caused by wind in the course of which much *chin* liquid is lost due to perspiration and thereby [*yang*] influences, and still no food is brought into the stomach, how should the deficiency in *yang* [influence] be eliminated?

In addition there are still deficiencies which may have been caused by "guest influences" [*k'o-ch'i*] or erroneous uses of drugs. In such cases, as a rule, the respiratory realm of one's body is purified [*ch'ing-fei*] and the blood is stopped [*chih-hsüeh*], in order to avoid a complete exhaustion of the *yang* [influences]. In any event an insufficient transformation [of influences from outside] through the fire [in the organism] is the basic cause here. Among all the mistakes committed by physicians with their patients, none equals in gravity those committed in this area.

How could I refrain from using all my strength to make all those contemporaries who are still confused and have not yet acquired the right knowledge receptive [to this knowledge].

[*Sixth*] *warning: Accepting heterodox teachings as one's model*—To a man who lives true to the principles, it will always be disconcerting to submit to deviant theories. Yet in the core of their works the men of letters advance at times toward heterodox areas. For a long time it has been observed that in the technical literature numerous medical treatises of a magical character have appeared. It is said there, for example, that a person who looks at the *kao-huang* area of the body knows immediately that this specific disease cannot be cured;[70] or that someone drinks the *shang-ch'ih* water and then immediately recognizes the congestions in all five granaries of the body [*wu-tsang*].[71] Absurd as the talking [of these physicians] may be, it is nevertheless conducive to spreading [the rumor] that they display supernatural powers in their professional activity. Quite contrary to those who form images of a man out of straw in order to cast out spirits [in a mysterious way], these people display their containers for drugs and openly practice their art to deceive the public. All kinds of

70. Cf. note 55.
71. An allusion to the way in which Pien Ch'io attained his knowledge. *Shih-chi,* PNP, ch. 105, p. 1023; Bridgman, "La médecine dans la Chine antique," pp. 17–18.

procedures are used to gain popularity. Yet even among the dullest in the country, everyone knows that he is dealing here with deception. This applies especially to the theory according to which one is to limit one's clothing during the winter months and is to expose oneself to the influence of summer heat. Truly this is the greatest public deception! In its very origin heat represents a formless influence. Yet it can supposedly be stored in a trunk like clothes, without disappearing during the months of winter. And whoever then "puts it on" is said to be protected from the cold and in no need of clothes!

Those who merely mimic others normally make even greater mistakes by their mimicking [than the authors of such theories], yet they are nevertheless firmly convinced that they have arrived at full agreement with the people in dark antiquity.

Such [nonsense as the theory described before] is really conducive to making those who truly grasp the principles [of medicine] laugh so hard that they have to hold their sides.

[*Seventh*] *warning: To treat noble and common patients alike*—In medicine a distinction is made between noble patients [*kao-liang;* literally, "grain"] and common people [*li-huo;* literally, "weeds"].

The reason for this lies in the development of numerous different [medical] traditions which deviate from each other in their preferences. It is difficult to compare these traditions with each other and to assess which is worse and which is better.

Those [physicians] who have adapted their practice to nobility focus exclusively on [exotic drugs] such as cinnamon and thereby gain a name for themselves all over the world. Those [physicans] who are familiar with [the] peculiarities of the common people consider [common drugs such as] orange peel as advantageous.

It is difficult to be successful in the treatment of the nobility. Here it is a matter of supporting the tender and fragile. [They suffer mainly from] a persistent chronic congestion in the upper [part of their body] and from a decline of their potency in the lower [part of their body]. If evil influences [*hsieh*] from outside are added to this, only ginseng but no [drugs with] active medicinal strength can bring relief.

Contrary to this the diseases of the common people are all easy to heal. Since the body [of these people] is built strong and flexible, harmful influences which have penetrated from the outside can be dispersed rapidly and those which develop from within can be attacked with strong medicaments. If damage due to exhaustion has occurred, one dose of the drug *pai-shu* will suffice to induce the effectiveness of all kinds of invigoration. Given the case now that a nobleman calls for a physician [of the common people] who has not yet attained any competency in [the medical needs of this social level], this physician will unavoidably be very nervous. Assuming a [patient from] the common people asks for a cure which is suitable for the nobility, this will certainly endanger his state of health. The reason for this lies in the fact that every person is enmeshed in the conditions of his life. It is simply impossible to take recourse to certain measures and thereby plan one's own fortune in advance.

[*Eighth*] *warning: To change one's attitude toward rich and poor*—Pien Ch'io has listed six circumstances in which no treatment is to be given. One of these is as follows: "To consider the body unimportant and to value material possessions highly." I have arrived at the conclusion that by this the disrespect is meant which the patients have for their own bodies. Yet why should I not carry out any treatment for this reason? That people are miserly lies in their nature. If I, however, use their reluctance to pay as an occasion to reject someone, this would imply that the diseases and pains of the poor people would be passed over without any further questions. Those who have acquired the abilities of a Hsien Yüan and a Ch'i Po[72] feel responsible for helping others, so as to be of use to them. What reason would there be to desire material gain? Admittedly the fees which the common people can hand to [the physician] are minimal; yet one should keep in mind how difficult it is for [these people] just to raise this small sum. Therefore one should take the greatest pains to carry out treatment. It is fully out of the question to send someone away, merely because he lacks the means! Whoever acts in this manner thwarts any thought with [these people] to come later on.

But those who have belonged to the aristocracy for generations, deliberately show poor manners [to the physician, when it is a question of rewards]. In this situation one has to be very discreet!

72. Legendary ancestors of the theoretical foundations of the medical philosophy of systematic correspondence: the Yellow Emperor Hsien Yüan Huang-ti and his minister Ch'i Po.

[*Ninth*] *warning: To exploit situations when others are in danger, to accept* [*rewards*] *without justification*—It is already immoral to accept [rewards] to which one is not entitled; it is however especially reprehensible if [someone else's] dangerous situation is exploited [for this]. Even if one has merited to fortify the heavens and to purify the sun, every good deed in one's life will be darkened and transformed into something bad, if one but once commits such an offense. Every unexpected happening is founded in this [fact], because whoever acts just as it pleases him will be successful [only by luck], yet otherwise only make mistakes.

Yet where a physician has proved his merit, it does no harm to accept [rewards]. In such a case he comforts the patient by his acceptance [of a reward]. Therefore the physician should accept [rewards] under such circumstances. However if he does not delight the patient by accepting, he should not take anything. To accept or not to accept therefore underlies well-defined limits; it is hardly becoming to someone who intends to practice humaneness, to exploit the dangerous situation [of others] in order to enrich himself ruthlessly.

A man can fill thousands of chests and accumulate them, still one day the end of his life will draw near. No one has ever heard of a member of the following generation being able to continue [his predecessor's] professional affairs without harm and at the same time increase the [accumulated] goods. Therefore an old proverb says: "A renowned physician does not have any successors." Indeed it is so!

[*Tenth*] *warning: Critique on colleagues*—Whoever is active in the field of technical skills [*i*] depends on a communicative exchange with his colleagues. True friendship should be a duty, especially for those who devote themselves to medicine. Because from this develops the merit of mutual assistance and the benefit of close collaboration.

Nowadays, however, colleagues have sold themselves to profit as the basis of their activity. Therefore it happens frequently that they have to rely on the power of exaggerated self-recommendations.

The cause [for this phenomenon] seems to lie in the fact that the families of the rich are not willing to trust in only a single physician. Consequently it [has] frequently happened that many different treatments [have] failed to succeed. The [custom of trusting several physicians at the same time] has spread to the lower levels of the population. Therefore it is necessary [if one is called in in such a situation] to analyze first whether the case in question is hopeless. If this is the case, then it is worthwhile to withdraw with many excuses. Wherever the vital strengths do not flourish, and yet a possibility to help can still be found, one should avoid looking at the prescriptions applied [by physicians called in] previously and discussing the drugs involved. Otherwise a physician inevitably puts impediments in his own way and contrary [to his actual intention] burdens himself with a heap of additional troubles. In such critical moments the physician has to explain [to the patient] that he is willing to save his life from death. In this manner it can be accomplished that no one of the physicians consulted before or after him accuses [the other].

Yet there are also occasions on which a physician has to collect all the prescriptions made use of so far and to discuss the respective procedures of the treatment, and on which it is but appropriate to adapt himself with his own prescriptions to the mass [of other physicians], because he neither can nor desires to accept the responsibility of developing an individual opinion. Whoever is not mislead by greed in such a situation can withdraw, and has nothing to do any more with the matter. For no one has ever heard yet that several physicians were able to restore a patient's health to the full in the course of a day.

Everywhere gossip is exchanged. When colleagues meet their conversation frequently takes this turn. They say, though, that such talk is without any ulterior motives, yet who can determine whether [this gossip] does not represent incorrect behavior after all? "Many words bring about many defeats," this was the first and most important rule of caution of the barbarians of Chin. Take it to heart![73]□

Following Chang Lu's very detailed ethics touching on numerous aspects of a physician's activity, I wish to cite again several prefaces containing statements, as marginal notes, which throw light on the tendencies toward professionalization and on the

73. Chang Lu, *Chang-shih i-t'ung,* "Shih-wan lao-jen i-men shih-chieh," pp. 1a–2a; this paragraph on ethics was not included in the 1963 reprint of the *Chang-shih i-t'ung* in Shanghai, which is otherwise complete.

levels of professionalization already attained by the different groups participating in the conflict represented here.

Nien Hsi-yao (fl. A.D. 1725), a onetime civil servant in the public works ministry, was the author of various medical works. In the first lines of the preface to the *Chi-yen liang-fang,* his collection of formulas for prescriptions, he briefly but clearly expressed his contempt for the physicians of his time who accepted money:

□ The physicians of antiquity practiced on the basis of solid studies to assist humanity. Nowadays physicians look for gain on the basis of no studies and enrich their own family. These two attitudes express the difference between noble and common people.[74]□

Further Efforts to Upgrade the Moral Value of Professional Healing

Authors of the eighteenth century very frequently resorted to parallels between the potential danger of drugs and the potential danger of soldiers, probably with the intention of escaping Chu Hsi's verdict that medicine was a "petty teaching." This despite the fact that Chu Hsi's statements were more than five centuries old. In the introduction which follows, composed in 1738 by Ling Chih-t'iao for the *Liang-p'eng hui-chi,* a collection of formulas for prescriptions by Sun Wei (fl. A.D. 1738–40), the author points to the vital significance of medical resources by comparison to the military.

□ In this world there are soliders to kill men. Yet if they are put into action wisely, the world will not have to suffer from their harmful influence. Quite on the contrary, they will then be apt to preserve the lives of the people. Medicine is in the world to preserve the lives of the people. Yet if it is not used skillfully, the world will have to suffer under its harmful influence. Quite contrary to its actual purpose, it will then be apt to kill people.

A forearm has to have been broken three times and then only will it be a strong forearm. An upper arm has to have been broken nine times, then only will it be a strong upper arm.

74. Nien Hsi-yao, *Chi-yen liang-fang,* preface by Nien Hsi-yao, pp. 1a–1b, in Nien Hsi-yao, *Ching-yen szu-chung.*

At all events medicine has to be taken for something difficult and considered very important. The proverb says: "It is a waste of paper to study books; it is a waste of man to study medicine." Indeed if a physician does not proceed with the greatest skill in his practice, but considers [the occupation with] life and death a pastime, how then can one still tolerate to speak about the principles of medicine?[75]□

Huang Yüan-yü (fl. A.D. 1755) had a very special reason to complain about the unsatisfactory situation in the medicine of his time. He had passed the first examinations for the career of a Confucian civil servant and had graduated as a *hsiu-ts'ai,* when a "common physician" injured his eyes. After this Huang Yüan-yü turned to the study of medicine and wrote numerous medical works. He began the preface to his *Szu-sheng hsüan-shu* in the following manner:

□ We have not yet come to the point that heaven only gives life, and does not take life. Sometimes it kills by means of soldiers or times of famine, in other cases through epidemics. Can we blame heaven for this? What we face here is certainly an act of heaven, but does not man too share the guilt? Soldiers and famines do not necessarily kill men, but there simply are no good administrators in the world. Epidemics too do not necessarily have to kill men, yet likewise there simply are no good physicians. When a minister is incapable, his offence is slight. Yet if a physician is not able, his offence is great. Since the times of the Wei [220–265] and the Chin [265–420] dynasties many people have lost their lives through epidemics. Although there are thousands of books on these problems and hundred thousands of people who were guided by them, diseases still are something families cannot avoid, and drugs are found in every household. This is deeply regrettable![76]□

Not much later we encounter another work in whose various prefaces, dating from 1766, the different authors express the efforts of practicing physicians toward professionalization in a formulated ethics. From several remarks the conclusion can be

---

75. Sun Wei, *Liang-p'eng hui-chi,* preface by Ling Chih-t'iao, p. 1a.
76. Huang Yüan-yü, *Szu-sheng hsüan-shu,* preface by Huang Yüan-yü, p. 1a, in Huang Yüan-yü, *Huang-shih i-shu pa-chung.*

drawn that these are physicians who felt linked to Confucianism. They attached importance to raising the value of medical resources in the public opinion which, at that time, was conditioned by the Confucian point of view. The little progress in regards to the conservative forces becomes apparent from the arguments. which did not change for so many centuries. From the text presented here, as also from some earlier texts on formulated ethics, it .follows that the professionalization of the freely practicing physicians had advanced further among the people than among the conservative dogmatists of the official ruling ideology; against them, obviously, arguments like· the following ones were still valid:

□ The great virtue of heaven and earth consists in the generation of life. Physicians assist heaven and earth with the generation of life. The three rulers of antiquity[77] regretted that the people entrusted to them were subject to an early death. Therefore they made use of various ideograms, in order to spell out the moving powers behind the rhythmical decrease and increase of *yin* and *yang*. They distinguished the radiations of temperature and the tastes in order to explain the principles of the reciprocal generation and overcoming of the Five Phases. They composed the *Ling-shu* and the *Su-wen,* in order to lay the groundwork of a medicine for all eternity. How splendid! How perfect! Not even the embryo in the body of a mother experiences so much humaneness and compassion! And even from among the most genuine sages, who could equal such examples?

In every century Hsien Yüan and Ch'i Po were succeeded by scholars with enlightened knowledge who fathomed the principles [which had been explained by the three rulers] and attained to a full understanding of them.[78]□

□ Men in antiquity adhered to three modes of conduct which had been allotted everlasting appreciation: proof of virtue [*li-te*], obtaining of merit [*li-kung*] and formulating a teaching [*li-yen*]. Although it may seem that we have here a three-part division, all

---

77. T'ai Hao Fu Hsi, Hsien Yüan Huang-ti and Shen-nung Yen-ti.

78. Yeh Kuei, *Lin-cheng chih-nan i-an,* preface by Shao Hsin, p. 1a; the author of the *Lin-cheng chih-nan i-an* is Hua Nan-t'ien, who published it under the name of the famous physician Yeh Kuei (*tzu* name: T'ien-shih). Yeh Kuei himself did not write a single work.

this is based on one single principle, namely that it is considered to be most important to assist the people. [The problem of] life and death is considered of vital importance by those who help the people.

And among all that is within the power of the most simple educated man to free his fellow men from [their fears concerning] life and death, there is nothing comparable to medicine.

A good physician does not live on earth to praise his own fame and to strive for profit. In this way he gives proof of his virtue. He brings creation under his control and has patients who are seriously ill rise again. Thereby he earns his merit. He explains what is not understood and composes literature of prescriptions. In this way he formulates his teaching. In the practice of one single profession, all three benefits are thus perfectly joined.

Who would not consider this relationship between medicine and the world important and splendid! For this reason the sages and rulers of antiquity distinguished between *yin* and *yang*, discerned the radiations of temperature and the tastes [of drugs] and composed the *Huang-ti nei-ching*. They introduced humaneness and compassion which are everlasting, so as to open the doors for a long life of the people. Their excellent writings, such as the *I-ching*, the *Pen-ts'ao*, the *Ling-shu*, and the *Su-wen* are splendid like the sun and the stars; these are documents which will not perish in all eternity.

For centuries to come exemplary people studied, in great detail, the principles put down in these works with the hope that each man would attain a level marked by humaneness and long life. Yet they did not compare to those who professionally practiced [those principles] in later generations. To the degree in which these people demonstrated their willingness and kept their attitude, the principles of heaven joined the aspirations of humanity.

Although Fan Wen-cheng kung [A.D. 989–1052] did not practice medicine himself, his statement "Whoever has no chance to work as a good administrator, may work as a good physician" clearly expresses the frame of mind of charitable assistance. A proverb says to this: "If a graduate of the first class [to whom the future of a Confucian civil service career is open] practices medicine, this is as if one preserved fresh vegetables [and put them aside rather than eating them]." This expresses the contempt for medical practice of those who see in it merely a means to gain clothing and food.

[A physician] who keeps an attitude of charitable assistance will irresistibly progress in his knowledge and in his practice to an ever higher and more brilliant realm from day to day.

[A physician] who is only concerned about the acquisition of clothing and food will ultimately remain caught up in common knowledge. Herein we find an expression of the difference between the principles of heaven and the aspirations of mankind; between community and selfishness.[79]□

□ The principles of the use of drugs resemble those of the employment of soldiers: the decision over life and death is made in the short span of time between two breaths. Therefore it is not easy to discuss this topic.

In the military there are writings and statutes. For the formulas of prescriptions there are rules and measures. [In war] the time demands progress or retreat; in [medical treatment] a single case [may result in] success or failure. [On the battlefield] the changes of wind and clouds are minutely observed; [at a patient's bedside] one knows the peculiarities of herbs and trees. The stimulating force [which is hidden behind all these phenomena] is highly ingenious. How could anyone speak of a "petty teaching" [*hsiao-tao*] in this connection! Even though I am not wise, I secretly admire what Fan Wen-cheng kung has said.[80]□

Chang Jen, the author of a preface dating from 1778 to Wan Ch'üan's *Wan Mi-chai shu,* also evidently felt the need to assert the value of medical resources for the concrete fulfillment of the Confucian values, such as "humaneness":

□ The principle of medicine is the principle of humaneness. Its basis is innate compassion, and help is its duty. I remember that my ancestors who served as governors in the frontier regions strove exclusively to keep men alive.[81]□

79. Yeh Kuei, *Lin-cheng chih-nan i-an,* preface by Hua Nan-t'ien, pp. 1a–1b.

80. Ibid., preface by Kao Mei, p. 1a.

81. Wan Ch'üan, *Wan Mi-chai i-hsüeh ts'ung-shu,* preface by Chang Jen, p. 1a.

We know little about Huai Yüan, the author of the *Ku-chin i-ch'e,* dating from the year 1808. We know only that he had prepared for a Confucian career in his youth; that he ultimately ceased to pursue this career any further for reasons which his biographers do not tell us; and that he then devoted himself to the study of medicine. From his statements, in a separate section of his book entitled "warnings for physicians" (*"I-chen"*), it follows that he advocated the values of the Confucian medical scholars. Some dimensions of his ethics are the awareness of a great responsibility, the demand for the greatest conscientiousness possible, and the emphasis on medicine as applied humaneness. Huai Yüan explained further that he acted as a representative of the patients and their families. In an understanding of professionalization as the transfer of primary medical resources from family possession and control into the hands of a third group, this statement has special significance.

Huai Yüan attacked those who "follow fashionable tendencies." As I wrote in the introduction, both the peculiarity of medical resources and the fact that several groups compete for the "secondary" resources in medicine represent a progressive factor, which may stimulate the search for ever new and more perfect "primary" resources in medicine. On several occasions, earlier authors had cautioned against "heterodox" ideas and theories. We may consider these, as well as the "fashionable tendencies" over which Huai Yüan had to worry, to be continuous efforts by practitioners and theoreticians to expand, if not to overcome, both the theoretical foundations represented in the *Huang-ti nei-ching* and the officially recognized framework of medicine. These attempts at expansion proved to be extremely difficult as long as the Confucian doctrine, which shared the basic concepts of this medicine, dominated the public domain of Chinese society. As a consequence those new "primary" resources in medicine which were apt to question the old foundations did not receive the public interest that would have been needed to support their distribution.

Closely connected to this tendency is the fact that leading figures among the Confucians thwarted the circulation of medical discoveries from the West which were brought to their attention by Jesuit scholars. The decision makers in the old China were obviously fully aware that cultural ecology causes changes to entail more or less foreseeable consequences in many other areas, even if they take place in a seemingly highly independent domain.

In his statements Huai Yüan placed a great value on prognosis. In this he can be paralleled with Chu Hui-ming (ca. A.D. 1590) and Chang Lu (A.D. 1627–1707), both of whose way of life closely resembled that of Huai Yüan. He saw only two reasons for the treatment of a hopeless case: emotional ties with the specific patient and greed. Huai Yüan rejected both. He thereby separated himself from a broad area of possible "secondary" resources. The text of Huai Yüan's ethics is as follows:

□ *WARNING TO PHYSICIANS*

Treatment—In medical practice one cannot act at one's own discretion. Patients entrust [physicians with the decision over their] life and their death, and our own responsibility is based on the principle of a requital later on.

Life is the most important element in the world. Once it has been placed in my hands, the use of supplementing and draining drugs, of cold and warm radiations of temperature [*hsing*],[82] and of tastes, of herbs and trees with a mild or a marked madicinal potency, has to raise those who are laid down, has to confer flesh to the bones and once more endow the weak with strength. A physician who takes the privilege to create into his hand in such a way will live up to it. However if he carries out superficial examinations and is not perfectly versed in knowledge, so that small mistakes cannot be avoided, he harms himself by harming others. Because there is no difference between the fathers and mothers, wives and children of other people and myself, how could I be able to bear their loud wailing, when the patient cannot be saved any more and his life is exhausted?

When a physician faces a patient, this requires a greater effort than a confrontation with an enemy. Whoever plans the strategy in the field quarters and then gains victories which extend far beyond a thousand miles is a good general. A good physician, however, is someone who is capable of expelling the two demons from their place of refuge in the short span of time between two breaths.[83] He

82. Since K'ou Tsung-shih (fl. A.D. 1116) the term *hsing* has been used with the meaning "temperature radiation" (of a drug after its intake into one's body) by various authors, instead of the more common term *ch'i*. Cf. K'ou Tsung-shih, *Pen-ts'ao yen-i,* ch. 1, p. 7; a translation of the specific section can be found in Unschuld, *Pen-ts'ao,* p. 84.

83. The *kao-huang* region is meant here; cf. note 55.

carefully observes the coloring [in the appearance of the patient] and alertly discerns his pitch and his vocal expressions. He shows mental absorption when feeling the pulse and diagnoses the symptoms in detail. Thus he takes into consideration what is available and where there are deficiencies; he searches for the causes and considers the consequences. He knows the normal and understands the changes. In this manner he helps in every case and never harms. His activity is useful and is in no case injurious. [A physician] who is well-balanced within himself and is not angry with others accumulates merits which will be registered in another world, and can stand aloof from accusations.

Oh yes! It is very difficult to speak about this topic!

Moral principles—In its origin medicine is applied humaneness. To see other people suffer rouses compassion and pity within oneself. Their trust and hope are infinite. Who should help them, if not I?

Mr. Tung Ch'en-fei used to tell me, in cases where medicinal drugs and chemical preparations show their effectiveness only slowly and reluctantly during the treatment of a disease, a person's attitude itself creates a wonderful effect. It is important to know that it is not so much a matter of speed and effectiveness of medicinal drugs and chemical preparations. For if the physician's own attitude is not genuine, he carries out superficial observations and deficient examinations. How could one recognize the course of a disease under these circumstances and get it under control to such an extent that it follows our calculations in any event and does not elude them? Only when the attitude is fully developed, will the patient's pain coincide with one's own at the moment of danger. If [the patients'] fathers and mothers, their wives and children do not worry about them, I will be concerned about them in place of their relatives. When the ailing themselves cannot make any decisions, I will make them in their place. Up to their sleep and thoughts, their dreams and sensations, I always put myself in their place. Thus some will be saved who were at the edge of destruction, and others receive preventive protection because they are afraid of changes for the worse.

[A physician] plans in detail and thinks comprehensively. He observes a disease and takes precautions against it to avoid a second. He is glad over a success and yet he is aware that one cannot repose on this. While attacking another country, one's own country has to be protected as well, and when guarding [one's own country], already new plans for the next offensive have to be forged.

A compassionate attitude lies in peaceful composure. Thereby heaven and earth can be observed and demons and spirits recognized; an increase of ingenious enlightenment is the consequence. Those, however, who surrender to fashionable trends, do not carry out their practice conscientiously. They place themselves in the greatest light and make use of the need of others in order to appropriate their material goods to themselves. They are not concerned about the lives of men, but have only their own profit in mind. As far as they plan for their physical well-being, they may be successful with this conduct. How is it, however, with the reward in a future life and with later consequences [still during this life]? Whoever considers this and does not thereby perspire all over his body with fear, is not a human creature!

Character—A physician has to love and respect himself; only then will he, when he faces a grave disease, possess enough trust [in himself]. I have studied at great length and in any diagnosis of a disease I proceed with exactitude and conscientiousness; how could I carelessly acquit myself of that which others have entrusted to me and which I have promised them? Those however who have it as their aim to [attain success] by their flattering manners, go to the patients without being invited, only to give pleasure to these people. And with this their art is exhausted. Although some of them are able to treat insignificant diseases, they cannot cope with the difficult ones. Others are able to treat common ailments but not the unusual diseases. They frequently consider severe something that is unimportant and only [by their actions] they change the serious to true danger. Well yes, people in this land entrust their lives to such persons and then they receive but an insincere treatment!

Yet in view of these alternatives physicians should not be conceited. I see the suffering caused by a disease and am exclusively concerned about the elimination of the patient's suffering. There is hardly enough time to save a patient. How could I, therefore, take time to plan illicit conduct which is to yield me profit? Besides, regardless of whether he is rich and of high rank, or poor and considered to be low, or whether he lives in the quarters of the women, every patient has to consider the practicing physician a trustworthy person. [A physician] may examine the respectable without any further consideration. Yet if he meets with the disreputable, he is first to assure himself of all the details related to it before making a decision. Of course, the patient too has to report frankly and without any fear. Thereby it will be possible to give adequate treatment to every disease, and thus help is ensured. Therefore a physician has to prove stability in his character.

Understanding the principles [*li*]—The principles of medicine are inexhaustible and resemble those which mark a career in Confucian scholarship. For if one fails in the writing of literature, this means a waste of paper, and if one fails as a physician, this means a waste of people. What a grave overlapping!

For ages perhaps one or two people have had their knowledge since birth [*sheng-chih*]. But even Yen-ti had to sample the herbs and only then did he have any knowledge of them; and Hsien Yüan posed questions concerning the transportation channels [inside the body] before developing his understanding of them. If we read: "On high explore the heavenly signs, down below grasp the principles of the earth, and in the middle know the matters of men," how could [those two emperors] have attained to knowledge without carrying out this exploring and this grasping? Later on, then, one famous man after another made his appearance. And there was not one among them who did not examine the origins of all principles, or observe the sum of all things or grasp the peculiarity and the life of men in depth. Together with their abilities they thereby attained respect during their lifetimes, and their glory will be passed on throughout all ages. Yet those who do not equal [these famous men in their efforts to examine the principles], indeed do not attain the knowledge of the exemplary figures in antiquity. Because they do not engage in comprehensive studies, they rarely recognize the "middle" [these are the affairs of men]. If such people take care of the life of other people, only a few cases will end without misfortune. Therefore the exemplary men of the times gone by used to say: "After ten years of the study of books [one believes] that there is no incurable disease. After ten more years of the study of books [one is certain] that there is no curable disease." This is a true saying!

Decisions—If a man in medicine has a compassionate nature, we speak of humaneness. If a person in medicine has a compassionate and at the same time a hardhearted nature, we speak of enlightenment. Humaneness lies within oneself, enlightenment however is related to material things. If I am faced with the case of a disease which cannot be cured under any circumstances, and I attempt to save the patient in spite of this fact, I must have accumulated knowledge in regard to the "middle" [that is the affairs of men] and experience with similar cases in the past. Yet when I examine [the results of my attempts at saving], I will come to the conclusion that it does not correspond to my expectations. There was in fact no other possibility. Is it not better to decide immediately in such hopeless cases to give up the case? Two reasons are responsible for such decisions not being made. For one thing the emotional ties with relatives play a part. Because one cannot bear their loss, one thinks up a hundred plans to protect them, in the hope that ultimately one will fortunately lead to success. Yet thereby the physician merely causes the patient to be angry. The second reason for reluctance quickly to reject [the treatment of an incurable case] lies in the hope of great profit. In such cases magnanimous words are to cover everything, until chance will perhaps bring about a success. Yet thereby a physician attracts only slander. Therefore if in a situation of danger the physician has clearly recognized the course of the phenomena, he should preferably make the decision not to treat early, and not worry about profits and emotional ties.

Those people who do not understand the principles of the pulse and cannot calculate the course of a disease, and who therefore make wrong decisions about the weal and woe [of the respective patient], engage in base conduct. Their abilities do not suffice to make them eligible to number among those physicians able to make the decision to refuse the treatment of a case. Indeed by what means should they improve their image?[84]□

In 1821 Wang Yün wrote a preface to the medical book *I-hsüeh hui-hai* by Sun Te-jung. There is little biographical material on either one of the two men. With respect to medical ethics Wang Yün expressed himself as follows:

□ According to my knowledge it was the adherence to four virtues which helped our precursors to the mastery of medicine. These are determination, wisdom, restraint, and humaneness.

84. Huai Yüan, *Ku-chin i-ch'e*, "I-chen," in *Tseng-pu chen-pen i-shu chi-ch'eng*, ch. 7, pp. 153–6.

Since diseases frequently break out unexpectedly and spread, determination is needed. In order to extract the force of the medical ancestors from all the accessories, and so as not to submit to insignificant things, restraint is needed. In order to receive the best from all parts of the country and to decipher the secrets, wisdom is needed. In order to renounce glory and profit and to focus merely on the help to live, humaneness is needed.[85]□

The End of the Debate on Ethics:
Persistence of Social Conflict and Group Heterogeneity

We approach the end of the nineteenth century and with it the end of the debate on ethics in the Chinese medicine of the Confucian era.

In 1874 the civil servant and onetime provincial governor Li Han-chang (1821–99), a brother of the famous politician Li Hung-chang (1823–1901), wrote a preface to an older work by Shen Chin-ao (fl. A.D. 1773), with the title *Shen-shih tsun-sheng shu*. Shen Chin-ao was a graduate of the rank of a *chü-jen* who devoted himself predominantly to classical studies and only in his old age turned to medicine. There exists no information on Li Han-chang which would tell that he himself had any special relation to medicine. His biographers stress his greed during his career as a civil servant. Since Li Han-chang did not practice medicine, he focused on Confucian ideals, untroubled by the interests of practicing physicians. His preface treats primarily of two points. It contains a critique of contemporary physicians who failed to study the things a Confucian would consider worth knowing, and followed the "unbalanced" and even carried out experiments. In his discussion we clearly recognize the conflict which had developed as a consequence of the increasing influence of Western medicine and the very intensive dissipation of traditional Chinese medicine into numerous different traditions having diverging medical theories. The second point which Li Han-chang emphasizes in his preface again displays a good example of the relationship of Confucianism to medicine. Shen Chin-ao, whose *tzu* name was Ch'ien-lu, could serve as such an example:

□ Not too long ago the Confucian scholar Ku T'ing-lin [i.e., Ku Yen-wu, A.D. 1613–82] made the following statement: "The physicians of antiquity were able to give life back to men and

85. Sun Te-jung, *I-hsüeh hui-hai*, preface by Wang Yün, pp. 16b–17a.

were capable of killing men. Physicians today are neither capable of keeping men alive, nor are they able to kill men. They are solely capable of reducing man to a state which represents neither life nor death and which finally ends in death!'' Truly, this statement is not true only of physicians!

Although Ku T'ing-lin has pointed out the situation he has not explained the reason for it. One [reason] reads: one does not study. Another is: one gets lost in the unbalanced.

The principles of medicine are subtle. Without any understanding of the background of decrease and increase of *yin* and *yang* and the Five Phases a physician is insufficiently equipped to examine the origins of human diseases. Whoever does not envision clearly the states of inner and outer, as well as of plentitude and deficiency of influences in the five [bodily] granaries and in the [six] collection centers cannot recognize their slowness or hurry in their permanence or changes. Yet for the consideration and the execution of all stages of a treatment, a physician has to be able to examine and to recognize the symptoms!

If one composes prescriptions without considering a patient's particular circumstances, if one prepares medication and does not choose the right drugs, how could this not inevitably be harmful to the sick person? But even harder to understand are the phases of the macrocosm and the climatic influences, and even far more diverse in significance are the colors of the face and the variations of pulses. If one does not accumulate several decades of efforts in this respect, has not read and reread hundreds of books and applied a balanced and unbiased mind to [the subject], how can one penetrate but one single partial area so completely that it remains open to one in all clearness and without any doubt?

People today do not distinguish between the six types of pulses and are not familiar with the peculiarities of drugs. They begin to practice in the morning and already in the evening they write prescriptions. Then there are even such **persons** who cling to one single tradition like leeches. The cheap little plants of the morbid tradition of Miu Hsi-yung [seventeenth century][86] give the incentive to harm life, and the expensive herbs of the degenerated tradition of Chang Chieh-pin equally suffice to bring about a fast death. Yet their books fill a house up to the beams of its roof and

---

86. Frequently criticized author of numerous medical works; cf. Unschuld, *Pen-ts'ao*, p. 159.

their followers crowd around. The latter may begin their studies as free men, yet they finish them as slaves. They unite with those who have the same opinion as they themselves, and attack all those who hold a different opinion. They try out their incomprehensible prescriptions with thousands of human lives. All this depresses me deeply!

During the ruling period *ch'ien-lung* [A.D. 1736–95], Shen Ch'ien-lu from Hsi-shan, who had the honorable title of *hsiao-lien* ["full of piety and pure"], had the reputation of possessing extensive knowledge. Originally he had not studied any medicine. One day while reading the *Shih-chi* he accidentally stumbled upon the biography of Pien Ch'io and suddenly he sensed the meaninglessness of all his activities. Someone ridiculed him and said: "Ignorance brings a Confucian scholar to shame!" Whereupon he developed a very great effort. Everywhere he looked for books of prescriptions, and studied them for more than forty years. Finally he had reached his goal; late in his life he wrote the *Tsun-sheng shu* in seventy-two chapters.[87]□

Finally we will quote three texts from a work with the title *I-ts'ui ching-yen* by Hsü Yen-tso (fl. A.D. 1895). As little known as the author himself are the composers of a preface and an epilogue to the work, both dating from 1895. The preface was written by Chiang Shih, who wrote:

□ Medicine consists of humaneness and skill. Some master the skill and are wanting in humaneness. These are the greedy physicians. Others possess humaneness, yet they lack skill. These are the "common" physicians. Commonness and greed are apt to harm man. Already in antiquity, it was said: "If [in the event of an illness] no drugs at all are taken, the result will be the same as if one follows a mediocre physician!" We really have to be on our guard, because humaneness and skill are difficult to combine in medicine![88]□

Ho Ch'i-pin, the author of the epilogue, similarly expressed himself in the sense of the old Confucian ideals, according to which medical resources should be distributed among the posses-

87. Shen Chin-ao, *Shen-shih tsun-sheng shu,* preface by Li Han-chang, pp. 1a–3a.
88. Hsü Yen-tso, *I-ts'ui ching-yen,* preface by Chiang Shih, p. 1a.

sions of every family in such a way as to make the existence of medical experts in independent practices unnecessary. Yet at his time the transition of the resources into the hands of experts was already taken so much for granted that Ho Ch'i-pin could no longer deny the fact that medicine was used to earn money; neither could he any longer attack this development. He wrote:

☐ For the practice of medicine generally two reasons are given: these are to earn a living and to help one's fellow men.

Whoever wants to protect his body and guard it against diseases needs to possess some medical knowledge. Those who serve their parents and who intend to bring up their own family have to be especially versed in medicine.

How can it be said then that [medical practice] exists merely to make a living and to help one's fellow man?

When I was ten years old, I took the examinations for boys. I went through the hall of examinations twice. In my middle years I was frequently ill. Nowhere did I succeed.

My mother, who has died in the meantime, suffered from a chronic disease. Neither physicians nor drugs were able to help her in the course of the years. Finally she died, without having been able to get up once more. I am sensitive to the warnings of the past and want to exclaim with a sigh, in order to warn posterity: "Whoever intends to protect his body and wants to serve his relatives has to have medical knowledge!" Yet it is important to take into consideration that insufficient medical knowledge is worse than no knowledge at all.[89]☐

Hsü Yen-tso, the author of the work *I-tsui ching-yen,* wrote thirty-three short articles under the title "Admonitions with regard to physicians and drugs" ("*I yao chen-yen*"), from which the advanced degree of professionalization of the practicing physicians of his time becomes evident. The majority of these brief treatises deal with pharmacological or purely medical questions. I have chosen nine sections to represent those related to the themes treated here.

Besides the ethical dimensions taken from former times, the description of the patient-physician relationship is particularly impressive. Now at least in their literature the practitioners could

89. ¹Ibid., epilogue by Ho Ch'i-pin, p. 1a.

claim that the physician had such an exclusive control over the resources in his field that he was able to exalt himself like a "superhuman," or even like a Buddha, over non-members of his group. Who would dare to criticize such a being? To be sure, all of Hsü Yen-tso's warnings can be interpreted in favor of the patient, yet in the light of professionalization they contribute their part in the transfer of the control over medical resources into the hands of the particular interest groups: the patient is not to have any secrets anymore; the patient has to enter a relationship of trust with the physician, not only temporarily, but permanently; everyone is treated, regardless of whether he is rich or poor; the patient is to be isolated from the influences of his social environment, for discussions about the effectiveness of treatment and a possible critique could otherwise be the consequence. Of course these admonitions failed to obtain fulfillment, because only a professional organization founded on legal authority could have made them generally effective. Yet from the very demands which are expressed by Hsü Yen-tso, it is possible to recognize the success of the group of independently practicing physicians in their efforts toward professionalization. If we compare Hsü Yen-tso's statements with the earliest texts cited above, it appears that it is only a small step from his claims, the gradual emergence of which we have followed in this study over thirteen centuries, to the ethical codes put forth by physicians in our own current medical system. The difference lies mainly in the degree of their enactment.

Hsü Yen-tso argued as follows:

□ *ADMONITIONS WITH REGARD TO PHYSICIANS AND DRUGS*

The intentions of physicians are twofold. One consists in preserving human life, the other consists in making a profit. Should we not be cautious in view of these contrary tendencies?

Without a lofty attitude a man cannot be a physician. And how can he be able to help the world, if he is wanting in prudence? A lofty attitude enlightens by itself the principles [of life] and prudence guards against the desire for glory. If we can combine both elements we certainly do not have to be ashamed to be a student of Huang-ti and Ch'i Po! Yet if we consider eloquence an advantage, how can we then possess a lofty attitude! And if we consider success a matter of luck, how then can prudence be present!

Patients have expectations of the physician as they do of

superhuman beings or Buddha. The physicians save patients like rain arriving just in time after a long period of draught. This [relationship] has to be put down in rules. If physicians are willing to come to the patient early, his family is not to criticize [the physician] because of this. Formerly there was a saying: "If patients ask for a physician, they hope for the arrival of a superhuman." On no account are physicians to postpone their visit. Otherwise the entire family of the patient will be in sadness and fear, and will wait with sighs on the mats of the bed. This can only evoke the greatest compassion!

If physicians do not proceed with the utmost sincerity, they will not be able to recognize the causes of the disease. When sick people call for a physician and do not display the utmost sincerity, they will not be able to stimulate the physician to his fullest engagement. A proverb says: "Truly, sincerity brings one everywhere!" Physicians and patients should consider this very closely.

If a patient places his trust in a physician, he should develop this trust over a long period of time, and not on short notice. Those in whom I place my trust over a long period of time, I may choose under tranquil circumstances with a detached and cool mind. Faced with those, however, in whom I place my trust on short notice [in the case of a crisis], there arise doubts and confusion, because I act in haste and hurry, am involved in the situation and cannot remain objective anymore.

Whoever recommends a physician out of compassion for a patient should know this physician very well. Otherwise he displays the [emotional] attitude of a grandmother and not the [rational] attitude of humaneness. Because if we place our trust in errors and take drugs based on this, we will try in vain to affect with these the cause [of the disease]. Limited opinions simply are not enlightened opinions. The reason for a patient's finding his way back to happiness or becoming a victim of trouble has always been based on this.

Among men there are rich and high-ranking persons, as well as poor ones and those with a low reputation. Yet among patients there are not those and these, close ones and distant ones. The physician has to treat them all alike and is not to deviate from his attitude of indiscriminate help. I have come to know those [physicians] who consider rich and high-ranking people important and tremble with fear [when they confront them]. Wherever an invigorating treatment is advisable, they fear that it is inappropriate. Attack and defense seem to them too dangerous. Their drugs therefore lack the decisive factor of use at the right moment. In this way they only accomplish proofs of failure. Then I have met those [physicians] who despise the poor and lowly and conduct themselves pompously in addition. When they are to come in the morning, they are displeased with the early hour of the day; when they are called in the evening, they are infuriated at the late hour of the day. To calls which do not yield any profit they respond only with reluctance. They lack the eagerness to help men. Both types of conduct are not only wanting in every respect; the question comes to mind, what sort of conscience can such people have? In the Buddhist classics we read: "The whole world is equal." Physicians should be guided by this opinion.

If a rich person is ill for a year, he can generously have the treatment performed for one year and is willing to submit for one year to a period of rest. A poor man who falls ill for only one day will endanger his place of work within one day, and increases his debts for one day. Physicians who turn their attention only to those who live in abundance and do not extend their compassion to those who are in need in their life can hardly be considered helpful to humanity. In fact they are unscrupulous.

The treatment of patients is entrusted to a physician. Yet the patient's care is the duty of his own family. When the care of the sick is not good, one should not seek the blame exlusively in the failure of the physician. A patient only needs repose. Yet one always has to rebuke well-meaning visitors for filling the sickroom with their exclamations and for urging the patient to respond. Are his energies not going to be exhausted thereby and his mind confused? Visitors who intend to make inquiries about the well-being of the patient should consider this.[90]

Another short paragraph of Hsü Yen-tso's work offers insight into the fact that at the end of the nineteenth century Chinese physicians lacked an essential dimension of professionalization, namely an autonomous professional organization equipped with the right to license. Well beyond the end of the Confucian era, traditional Chinese physicians remained a non-homogeneous

90. Ibid., ch. 2, pp. 56b, 58b–60a, 61a, 63b–64a.

group which included practitioners of the most diverse training and skills. In addition to these there arrived in the last century Chinese physicians with Western training, whose levels of proficiency varied in a similar way. Therefore it is not surprising that in his efforts to distinguish the elite from the mass of his colleagues, Hsü Yen-tso once more took recourse to the term *yung-i* in order to point out those who did not correspond to his expectations:

☐ *COMMON PHYSICIANS [YUNG-I] KILL MEN*

Men rarely die from diseases, frequently they die from drugs. Those practicing today in the [medical] profession, exercise themselves at first in eloquence and with this they then kill men. It is truly deplorable that they become famous in this manner too![91]☐

That there was sufficient reason for suspicion against at least some of those physicians who offered their services to the general population in return for remuneration was shown by a small medical treatise entitled *Ch'uan-ya*. Chao Hsüeh-min (ca. A.D. 1730–1805), a scholar who is best known for his compiling of the *Pen-ts'ao kang mu shih-i* as a supplement to the famous Ming *materia medica, Pen-ts'ao kang mu*,[92] had interviewed an itinerant physician and had recorded this man's prescriptions, secret terminology and also his ethics. In the introductory section to the *Ch'uan-ya,* which did not find a publisher before 1851, Chao Hsüeh-min, while praising his informant's skills and prescriptions, denounced some of the ethics of which he became aware in the course of the interview. He especially referred to the practice of "planting" [*chung*] diseases in healthy persons in order to reap a profit from treating the resulting cases.[93]

For more than twelve centuries after an initial code of ethics had been written by Sun Szu-miao, numerous moral exhortations had been published by almost all the groups involved in health care in China. Yet the continued existence of practices such as "planting" diseases demonstrates that there is no dimension inherent in healing which would urge practitioners voluntarily to act in conformity with certain ethical standards. Explicitly recognized

91. Ibid., ch. 2, p. 24a.
92. Unschuld, *Pen-ts'ao,* pp. 143–46.
93. Chao Hsüeh-min, *Ch'uan-ya,* pp. 6–7; for an analysis of the treatise and for a translation of several of its sections see Paul U. Unschuld, "Das Ch'uan-ya und die Praxis chinesischer Landärzte im 18. Jahrhundert."

medical ethics as expressed in the texts quoted in the preceding pages are simply to be seen as a partial paradigm, designed and accepted by some in society out of conviction that the values proposed are good, and by others out of an understanding that enforcement of these values serves their interests. Still there is also a fourth group in our model (see p. 9), who are those who will follow a paradigm only under pressure. Whether in the case of Chinese explicitly recognized medical ethics the fourth group constituted a majority or a minority of all healers practising cannot be assessed any longer. In any case, at the end of the Confucian era Chinese society lacked an appropriate instrument to exert the necessary pressure to narrow the gap between explicitly recognized and tacitly recognized medical ethics.

three

Concluding Remarks

The texts of the formulated ethics of Chinese physicians during the Confucian era cited in the previous chapter offer us statements which are valuable in many ways.

In the first place they can be considered an example of paradigms used by various interest groups who were in conflict over the distribution of resources. In this case they represent recourse to the partial paradigm "ethics" to influence the distribution of resources in the field of medicine. The groups in this conflict were Confucian dogmatists, Confucian official physicians, Confucian medical scholars outside the medical civil service, independently practicing physicians and, finally, lay people outside Confucian training. In the preceding presentation the significance of the other groups, such as the shamans or the priests, and also simply that of the population of laymen, has admittedly been neglected and is expressed only in a few marginal remarks in the texts. Nevertheless it should be kept in mind that a series of Confucian-oriented texts represented the advocacy of the interests of the general public.

The "primary" and "secondary" resources of medicine were the object of the conflict presented here. Originally the control and possession of these resources, as far as they were available, were in the hands of the population, without there being any visible experts. In ancient China we can observe the process of a rising group endeavoring to legitimate the share of the medical resources which they had already secured, and to increase this share decisively. By "a rising group" we mean a group in the process of professionalizing itself, namely the intellectual elite of the independently practicing physicians. In our texts this group was opposed by the orthodox Confucians, whose aim was to prevent the rise of potentially influential groups with specialized knowledge. In their arguments these Confucians insisted on the claim that medical resources had to remain distributed equally among the general public. At the same time, however, additional groups appeared within Confucianism, who endeavored to have control and possession of medical resources restricted to this ruling class of Confucians, and who themselves fought for the mandate to administer these resources.

In a more recent time the problem of expertise, of which the decision makers in Confucian society were well aware, has again become a central theme in the political conflicts over health policy in societies of such different organization as those of communist China and of some industrial nations in the West. In Confucian society the attempt was made (although it did not become reality) to give each individual so much medical training that medical care within the family would be guaranteed, and beyond this to put medical practice outside the limitations of the family into the hands of civil servants, who were to practice only on the basis of a service orientation and not on the basis of profit maximization. This notion of a nationalized health-care system, in which one has but to exchange the terms "within the family" and "outside the family" for "primary" and "secondary/tertiary" medical care, seems to be socialistic to a degree that it does not have to fear a comparison with current notions in China. The differences lie in the degree to which these superficially very similar concepts have materialized, and in the total social context in which they were formulated.

A positive statement made possible by a comparison of the concepts only has therefore little more meaning than, for instance, the observation that in both Confucian and communist China the walls of houses are erected vertically. What is significant is a negative statement to which the preceding comparison points, namely that it is questionable to draw premature conclusions about the total social structure from the concepts of a particular institution.

The texts on the ethics debate show that in ancient China all the participating groups designed models of explanation about the origin and the best patterns of distribution of primary medical resources, and proposed them as a formulated ethics. In this context I have shown that the three terms "model of explanation," "paradigm," and "ideology," are interchangeable. I have thereby approached the view of sociology of knowledge, which considers ideology as primarily free of value and not per se as a "falsehood," "lie" or "perceptive teaching." Beyond this I have adopted the point of view that ideologies are not only linked to the interests of the ruling class—that is to say, the groups which are in an advantageous position of control and possession of resources—but that it is just as likely for them to be applied by those groups who endeavor to change the distribution of resources which correspond to their interests in their own favor. In this connection it has been necessary to define the terms "progressive" and "conservative" completely free of value, that is to say, "progressive" as the "endeavor of a group to increase their share of certain resources available in the society," and "conservative" as the "endeavor of a group to retain their established share in certain resources available in the society."

Besides the explanatory content, it is the values which constitute the central dimension of the paradigms. In the formulated ethics of our texts we were dealing with a partial paradigm which is related exclusively to the realm of medicine, and which was to change or maintain the pattern of distribution of the resources only within this field (irrespective of the possibility of far-reaching consequences caused by eventual changes). In many cases it is characteristic of the application of these partial paradigms that at least one part, if not all, of the values employed are taken from the comprehensive paradigm which dominates in the specific society. Besides the explanatory character of ideologies, it is the values which are to exercise the strongest psychological stimulation for the target groups to open themselves to the specific ideology and to support the group which advocates it. The significance of the values is so great that even the creators of new ideologies which radically depart from already established ideologies frequently abstain from the formulation of their own value terms [*Wertworte*], and instead accept already introduced value terms with a newly defined meaning.

A further statement made possible by the texts introduced in this study refers to the actual process of the professionalization of the independently practicing healers in imperial China. Here we have to point out that generalizing statements, such as those about the inferior social status of physicians in old China, as well as opposite assertions, should be considered as obsolete. *The Chinese physician as a definable entity did not exist.*[1]

The medical resources available in China were widely distributed among many persons. Up to this century these have included shamans, Buddhist priests, Taoist hermits, Confucian scholars, itinerant physicians, established physicians, "laymen" with medical knowledge (gained from experience or obtained through family tradition), midwives, and many others. They all were "Chinese physicians" when they practiced medicine, and the conflict over the distribution of medical resources concerned all of these people equally.

From the content of our texts we can observe the tendency that, in spite of all Confucian efforts to the contrary, the control and possession of "primary" and consequently also of "secondary" medical resources passed more and more into the hands of the independently practicing physicians.

In the light of a cross-cultural comparison, the Chinese debate over ethics teaches us that there is far-reaching similarity between it and the course of medical professionalization in the Occident. It was not the results which were at all times the same; the similarity lies rather in the dimensions of the ethics which were recognized and conceptualized by the core group of independently practicing physicians. This occurred in order to change the distribution of resources in their favor, while at the same time promoting the

1. In this context it is difficult to agree with Needham's analysis of the social situation of the different groups which shared the control and possession of medical resources in ancient China, when he writes: "The whole history of the social position of doctors in China might be summarized as the passage from the *wu*, a sort of technological servitor, to the *shih*, a particular kind of scholar, clad in the full dignity of the Confucian intellectual, and not readily converted into anyone's instrument" (*Clerks and Craftsmen in China and the West*, p. 265).

protection needed for this change. The implications of this fact must be emphasized.

In the eyes of many who made comparisons, China was "entirely different." Only in more recent times, as a result of new methodological approaches, does the presumed singularity of the development of China begin to waver. We recognize now that under the veneer of singular culture were hidden the same processes and phenomena attendant on human conduct in the European culture of the past.

It would be too much to expect that such parallels of subsurface phenomena would everywhere provoke exactly corresponding cultural manifestations. On the contrary, every cultural realm produces certain characteristics which are peculiar to the ecological conditions. Here I broadly define "ecology" to mean "the entire network of concrete and abstract environmental conditions in which there is a more or less self-contained human society involved." This includes tangible phenomena such as available food, products of the soil, and climate and geographic conditions, as well as elusive elements such as the entire range of ideological influences to which the society is exposed.

Wolfram Eberhard has pointed out that a society given a wide, open countryside with a visible sky full of stars above it will develop different ideas and paradigms from, for instance, a society which passes its life in dense tropical forests which obstruct the view of the heavens.[2] Eberhard thereby showed the ecological conditioning of social characteristics. Yet the differences between cultures which develop from such peculiarities cannot delude us to the fact that, wherever man lives in communities or societies, he will also be preoccupied predominantly with the distribution and increase of those resources which are scarce and stand in some relationship to his pattern of need. The varying patterns according to which this process of distribution proceeds are certainly far more limited than one is apt to expect after a superficial observation of all the many cultures in the world. The variety lies in the ideas which are interwoven with these processes of distribution. They can be crude and obvious to the extent that they still display their purpose visibly; they can be refined and in their conclusions

2. Wolfram Eberhard, "Beiträge zur kosmologischen Spekulation Chinas in der Han Zeit," p. 1.

so far advanced from their original motivations that they develop their own measures, which have lost any connection with those motivations.

Returning to medical ethics, even though I observe that as a means of protection the formulated ethics has replaced prognosis, this does not at all mean that prognosis has disappeared in this function today. The contrary is the case. As a means of protection, and then also for the enhancement of the physician's reputation, prognosis is regaining an increased significance[3] at a time when there is more and more demand in the U.S. to give account for one's activity; be this for economic reasons, in order to ensure the best possible distribution of the financial resources at hand in the society, or be it to give expression to the patients' dissatisfaction.

The interpretation of ethics formulated by physicians which has been used as the basis for this present study is chiefly as a protective mechanism and a paradigm employed by members of the group of practicing physicians to convey a desired reality to the general public [the ethics of the Confucian dogmatists has to be considered a counter-reaction]. This particular interpretation can be extended to our present problems in medical ethics only under certain conditions, for instance when decisions have to be made as to access to kidney dialysis machines, as to the selection of donors for heart transplantations, or the maintaining of vestigial functions of human life.

Here we have to consider the following. The rising group of independently practicing physicians one or two millennia ago lived in a society with a comprehensive paradigm, the values of which, generally speaking, were established for long periods of time. Today the core group of physicians both represents a leading group in society, in regard to its status, and moves at the utmost front of a rapid scientific and technological progress into domains of human conduct which were unknown up to now and for which there are no established values. Therefore, the function of a for-mulated ethics for physicians today cannot solely lie in dem-

---

3. The notion of a "defensive medicine" which has developed in the U.S. may serve as an example for illustration of a renaissance of prognosis, in this case as a means of protection. Under the pressure of the steady increase of malpractice suits, some physicians in private practice have changed their policy and decline the treatment of cases where the outcome seems outside their control. Cf., for in-stance, E.H. Holles, "California Doctors Turn to 'Defensive Medicine' as Mal-practice Suits Rise."

onstrating that the said group is willing to subject itself to the values dominating in this society; the significance of this ethic has rather to lie foremost in creating these values in the frontier regions of medicine. The dimension of a creation of values has thus been added to the original protective and explicative functions.[4] Now it depends on the non-medical groups in society whether these new values, which are offered by today's core group of physicians as corresponding to the interests of this group, will permanently be accepted as generally valid, or rejected.

---

4. The creation of values has been and will also be necessary in the future in modern situations such as the selection of donors for organ transplantations, the allocation of scarce resources to preserve life (kidney dialysis machines, heart operations, and others) eugenic counselling, change of gender in infants, mass sterilization, artificial continuation of the life of newborn infants with grave deformations which will place them in continuing dependence, etc.

Glossary

Chai Liang 翟良
Chang Chan 張湛
Chang Chieh-pin 張介賓
Chang Jen 張任
Chang Kao 張杲
Chang Lu 張璐
Chang Ts'ung-cheng 張徒正
Chang Wei-jen 張惟任
Chao Hsüeh-min 趙學敏
Che-kung man-lu 折肱漫錄
chen 眞
Chen Ch'üan 甄權
Chen Li-yen 甄立言
Ch'en Meng-lei 陳夢雷
Ch'en Shih-kung 陳實功
ch'eng-shih 誠實
Ch'eng Yung-p'ei 程永培
chi (technology) 技

chi (technical activity) 伎
ch'i 氣
chi-i 技藝
chi-liu 技流
Ch'i Po 岐伯
Chi-yen liang-fang 集驗良方
Chia-i ching 甲乙經
Chiang Ch'ou 江疇
Chiang Shih 江史
Ch'ien-chin fang 千金方
Ch'ien-chin i-fang 千金翼方
chien-i 賤役
chih 直
ch'ih 尺
chih-hsüeh 止血
chin 津
Chin Meng-shih 金夢石
chin-shih 進士

123

ching 精

ch'ing-fei 清肺

chiu-shih 灸師

Chou-li 周禮

Chu Chen-heng 朱震亨

Chu Feng-hsiang 朱鳳翔

Chu Hsi 朱熹

Chu Hui-ming 朱惠明

chü-jen 舉人

Chu Kung 朱肱

Chu Lun 朱鑰

ch'üan 全

ch'uan-hsin 傳心

chuan-i 專醫

Ch'uan-ya 串雅

chün-i 軍醫

chung 種

chung-i 中醫

Chung-kuo i-hsüeh ta-tz'u-tien 中國醫學大辭典

chung-shu 忠恕

fa-je 發熱

fa-san 發散

Fan Chung-yen 范仲淹

fang-chi 方技

fang-chia 方家

fu 腑

fu-ch'i 伏氣

Fu Hsi, T'ai-hao 伏羲太昊

Han Mao 韓懋

Han-shih i-t'ung 韓氏醫通

Ho Ch'i-pin 何起濱

hsiao 小

hsiao ch'ai-hu 小柴胡

hsiao-hsüeh 小學

hsiao-lien 孝廉

hsiao-tao (petty teachings) 小道

hsiao-tao (drain) 消導

hsieh (evil influences) 邪

hsieh (reduce excess) 瀉

hsien-tao 仙道

hsing 性

hsiu-ts'ai 秀才

hsü 虛

Hsü Chih-ts'ang 許智藏

Hsü Ch'un-fu 徐春甫

Hsü i-shuo 續醫說

Hsü Ta-ch'un 徐大春

Hsü Yen-tso 徐延祚

hsüeh 血

Hsüeh Chi 薛己

Hua Nan-t'ien 華南田

Huai Yüan 懷遠

Huang Ch'eng-hao 黃承昊

Huang-fu Mi 皇甫謐

Huang-ti, Hsien Yüan 皇帝軒轅

Huang-ti nei-ching 黃帝內經

Huang Yüan-yü 黃元御

Hui-ch'ang i-p'in chi 會昌一品集

huo-ch'i 火齊

i (righteousness) 義

i (physician) 醫

i (technical skills) 藝

I-chen 醫箴

I-ching 易經
I-hsüeh hui-hai 醫學滙海
I-hsüeh ju-men 醫學入門
i-kung 醫工
I-kung pao-ying 醫功報應
i-shu 醫術
I-shuo 醫說
I-ts'ui ching-yen 醫粹精言
i-tuan 異端
I-wen chih 藝文志
I-yao chen yen 醫要箴言

jen 仁
jen-shu 仁術
ju 儒
ju-i 儒醫
Ju-men shih-ch'in 儒門事親
jung 榮

kao-huang 膏肓
kao-liang 膏粱
Kao Mei 高梅
Kao Pao-heng 高保衡
k'o-ch'i 客氣
Ko Ch'ien-sun 葛乾孫
Ko Ying-lei 葛應雷
k'ou 口
K'ou Tsung-shih 寇宗奭
Ku-chin i-ch'e 古今醫徹
Ku-chin i-t'ung ta-ch'üan
　古今醫統大全
Ku-chin t'u-shu chi-ch'eng
　古今圖書集成
Ku Yen-wu 雇炎武
kuan 關

kuei-chih t'ang 桂枝湯
Kung Hsin 龔信
Kung T'ing-hsien 龔廷賢
kuo-i 國醫
kuo-shou 國手

Lai Fu-yang 來復陽
Lao-tzu 老子
Lei-kung 雷公
li (interior) 裏
li (principle) 理
Li Ch'an 李梴
Li Chung-tzu 李中梓
Li Han-chang 李瀚章
Li Hung-chang 李鴻章
li-huo 藜霍
Li Kao 李杲
Li Kuang-ti 李光地
li-kung 立功
Li T'ao 李濤
li-te 立德
Li Te-yü 李德裕
li-yen 立言
liang 艮
liang-i 艮醫
Liang-p'eng hui-chi 艮朋彙集
Lin Ch'i-lung 林起龍
Lin I 林億
Ling Chih-t'iao 凌之調
ling-i 鈴醫
Ling-shu 靈樞
liu-chu 流注
liu-fu 六腑
Liu Ming-shu 劉銘恕
Lu Ch'i 陸圻

Lu Chih 陸贄
Lun ta-i ching-ch'eng
　論大醫精誠
Lun t'ai-i ching-ch'eng
　論太醫精誠
Lun-yü 論語

mai 脈
Mai-ching 脈經
mien-yao 綿藥
ming 明
ming-i (enlightened
　physicians) 明醫
ming-i (renowned physicians)
　名醫
Miu Hsi-yung 繆希雍

Nan-ching 難經
Nan-yang huo-jen shu
　南洋活人書
Nei-ching su-wen 內經素問
Nien Hsi-yao 年希堯

pai-shu 白朮
Pan Ku 班固
Pei-chi ch'ien-chin yao-fang
　備急千金要方
pen-ts'ao 本草
Pen-ts'ao kang mu 本草綱目
Pen-ts'ao kang mu shih-i
　本草綱目拾遺
Pen-ts'ao yen-i 本草衍義
piao 表
Pien Ch'io 扁鵲
pu 補

sai 塞
shan-kung 善工
shang-ch'ih 上池
shang-han 傷寒
Shang-han chun-sheng
　傷寒準繩
shang-ku sheng hsien
　上古聖賢
Shao Hsin 邵新
shen 神
Shen Chia-pen 沈家本
Shen Chin-ao 沈金鰲
Shen-nung, Yen-ti 神農炎帝
Shen-shih tsun-sheng shu
　沈氏尊生書
sheng-chih 生知
shih (excess) 實
shih (treatment failure) 矢
Shih-chi 史記
shih-ch'i 時氣
shih-ch'in 事親
shih-i 世醫
shih-p'o 師婆
Shih-wan lao-jen i-men
　shih-chieh 石頭老人醫門
　十戒
Shih-yao shen-shu 十藥神書
shu-hsüeh 俞穴
Shun-yü I 淳于意
Su Shih 蘇軾
Su-wen 素問
Sun Ch'i 孫奇
Sun Szu-miao 孫思邈
Sun Te-jung 孫德潤
Sun Wei 孫偉

Szu-k'u ch'üan-shu t'i-yao
四庫全書提要
Szu-ma Ch'ien 司馬遷
Szu-sheng hsüan-shu
四聖縣樞
szu-shih shang-han 四時傷寒

ta-i 大醫
t'ai-chi 太極
t'ai-i 太醫
t'ai-i yüan 太醫院
Tai Liang 戴艮
t'ai-shih kung 太史公
t'ai-yang 太陽
tan 丹
tao 道
tao-hsüeh 道學
tao-li 道理
T'ao Tsung-i 陶宗儀
te-i 德醫
Tou-chen ch'uan-hsin lu
痘疹傳心錄
tsang 臟
Tsang Mao-chung 臧懋中
Tso-ch'uan 左傳
ts'un 寸
tu 毒
tuan-kung t'ai-pao 端公太保

t'ung 通
tz'u 慈

Wai-k'o cheng-tsung 外科正宗
Wan Ch'üan 萬全
Wan Mi-chai shu 萬密齋書
Wan-ping hui-ch'un 萬病回春
Wang Hsi 王熙
Wang Huan 汪宦
Wang K'en-t'ang 王肯堂
Wang Yün 王鋆
wei (protective influences) 衛
wei (taste) 味
wu 巫
Wu Chung-hsi 吳重熹
wu-i 巫醫
wu-tsang 五臟

yang 陽
yeh-hsing pu-shih 夜行卜士
Yeh Kuei 葉桂
yin 陰
yin-te 隱德
ying 營
Yü Pien 愈辨
yün 運
yung 庸
yung-i 庸醫

Bibliography

1. Primary Sources

Chai Liang. *I-hsüeh ch'i-meng hui-pien.* N.p.: Wen-ch'eng t'ang, n.d. 醫學啓蒙彙編文盛堂

Chang Chieh-pin. *Chang-shih Ching-yo ch'üan-shu.* Shanghai: Chin-chang t'u-shu-chü, n.d. 張氏景岳全書上海錦章圖書局

Chang Kao. *I-shuo.* N.p., 1544. 醫說

Chang Lu. *Ch'ien-chin fang yen-i.* Shanghai: Sao-yeh shan-fang, 1801. 千金方衍義上海掃葉山房

——. *Chang-shih i-t'ung.* Shanghai: Chin-chang t'u-shu-chü, n.d. 張氏醫通上海錦章圖書局

——. *Chang-shih i-t'ung.* Shanghai: K'o-hsüeh chi-shu ch'u-pan-she, 1963. 張氏醫通上海科學技術出版社

Chao Hsüeh-min. *Ch'uan-ya.* Hongkong: Shih-yung ch'u-pan-she, 1957. 串雅香港實用出版社

Ch'en Meng-lei et al. *Ku-chin t'u-shu chi-ch'eng.* N.p.: Chung-hua shu-chü, n.d. 古今圖書集成中華書局

Ch'en Shih-kung. *Wai-k'o cheng-tsung.* Revised edition edited by Hsü Ta-ch'un. Shanghai: Hai-tso shu-chü, 1905. 外科正宗上海海左書局

Ch'eng Yung-p'ei, ed. *Liu-li chai i-shu shih-chung.* Canton: Ts'ang-hsiu t'ang, 1891. 六醴齋醫書十種廣州藏脩堂

Ch'iu Han-p'ing, ed. *Li-tai hsing-fa chih.* Changsha: Shang-wu yin-shu-kuan, 1938. 歷代刑法志長沙商務印書館

Chou-li, Szu-pu tsung-k'an edition. 周禮四部總刊
Chu Hsi. *Hsiao-hsüeh chi-ch'eng.* Kyoto: Fugetsu Shozaemon, 1658. 小學集成京都風月庄左衛門
─────. *Lun-yü chi-chu.* Taipei: Chung-hua ts'ung-shu wei-yüan-hui, 1958. 論語集註台北中華叢書委員會
─────. *Chu-tzu ch'üan-shu.* Edited by Li Kuang-ti. N.p.: Hung-tao t'ang, 1714. 朱子全書　宏道堂
Chu Lun. *Hui-min chü pen-ts'ao shih-chien.* Shanghai; Ch'ien-ch'ing t'ang, 1899. 惠民局本草詩箋上海千頃堂
Erh-shih-szu shih, edition *Po-na-pen* (PNP). 二十四史
Hsü Ch'un-fu. *Ku-chin i-t'ung ta-ch'üan.* N.p., 1570. 古今醫統大全
Hsü Yen-tso. *I-ts'ui ching-yen.* Canton: T'ieh-ju i-hsien, 1896. 醫粹精言，廣州鐵如意軒
Huai Yüan. *Ku-chin i-ch'e.* Taipei: Shih-chieh shu-chü, 1971. 古今醫徹台北世界書局
Huang Yüan-yü. *Huang-shih i-shu pa-chung.* Revised edition edited by Tso Chi-ming. N.p.: Wang-yün ts'ao-lu, 1862. 黃氏醫書八種望雲草廬
K'ou Tsung-shih. *Pen-ts'ao yen-i.* Shanghai: Shang-wu yin-shu-kuan, 1957. 本草衍義上海商務印書館
Kung T'ing-hsien. *Wan-ping hui-ch'un.* Shanghai: Ta-ch'eng shu-chü, 1925. 萬病回春上海大成書局
Li Ch'an. *I-hsüeh ju-men.* N.p., n.d. 醫學入門
Li T'ao. "Chung-kuo ti i-hsüeh tao-te-kuan." *Chung-hua i-hsüeh tsa-chih* 27, no. 11 (1941): 679–88. 中國的醫學道德觀中華醫學雜誌
Nien Hsi-yao. *Ching-yen szu-chung.* N.p.: Wu-liu chü, n.d. 經驗四種五柳居
Okanishi Tameto. *Sung i-ch'ien i-chi k'ao.* Taipei: Ku-t'ing shu-wu, 1967. 宋以前醫籍考台北古亭書屋
Shen Chia-pen, ed. *Yüan tien-chang.* N.p.: Hsiu-ting fa-lü-kuan, 1908. 元典章修訂法律館
Shen Chin-ao. *Shen-shih tsun-sheng shu.* Hupei: Ch'ung-wen shu-chü, 1874. 沈氏尊生書湖北崇文書局
Sun Szu-miao. *Ch'ien-chin i-fang.* Shanghai: Chiu-ching-chai shu-chuang, 1908. 千金翼方上海久敬齋書莊
Sun Te-jung. *I-hsüeh hui-hai.* N.p., 1826. 醫學滙海
Sun Wei. *Liang-p'eng hui-chi.* N.p.: K'ang-hui t'ang, 1738. 艮朋彙集康惠堂
Tamba Mototane. *Chung-kuo i-chi k'ao.* Peking: Jen-min wei-sheng ch'u-pan-she, 1956. 中國醫籍考北京人民衛生出版社
T'ao Tsung-i. *Cho-keng lu.* N.p., 1366. 輟耕錄
T'ung-chih t'iao-ko. Peking: Kuo-li Pei-p'ing t'u-shu-kuan, 1930. 通制條格北平國立北平圖書館
Wan Ch'üan. *Wan Mi-chai i-hsüeh ts'ung-shu.* N.p., n.d. 萬密齋醫學叢書

Wang K'en-t'ang. *Liu-k'o chun-sheng.* Shanghai: Hung-pao-chai shu-chü, 1923. 六科準繩上海鴻寶齋書局
Wu Chung-hsi, ed. *Yü-i shuang-pi.* N.p., 1909. 豫醫雙璧
Yeh Kuei. *Lin-cheng chih-nan i-an.* N.p., 1766. 臨證指南醫案

2. Secondary Sources

Biot, Edouard. *Le Tcheou-li.* Peking: Wen Tien Ko, 1940.

Bridgman, R.G. "La médecine dans la Chine antique." *Mélanges chinois et bouddhiques* 10 (1955): 1–213.

Eberhard, Wolfram. "Beiträge zur kosmologischen Spekulation Chinas in der Han-Zeit." *Baessler Archiv* 16, no. 1 (1933): 1–100.

Eichhorn, Werner. "Bemerkungen zum Aufstand des Chang Chio und zum Staate des Chang Lu." *Mitteilungen des Instituts für Orientforschungen der Deutschen Akademie der Wissenschaften* 3 (1955): 291–327.

Foster, George. "The Anatomy of Envy: A Study of Symbolic Behavior." *Current Anthropology* 3 (1972): 165–186.

Hallowell, Irving A. "Ojibwa world view and disease." In *Man's Image in Medicine and Anthropology,* edited by I. Galdston, pp. 258–315. New York: International Universities Press, 1963.

Hartwell, Robert M. "Financial Expertise, Examinations and the Formulation of Economic Policy in Northern Sung China." *Journal of Asian Studies* 30, no. 2 (1971): 281–314.

Holles, E.H. "California Doctors Turn to 'Defensive Medicine' as Malpractice Suits Rise." *New York Times,* 27 January 1974, p. 20.

Lee, T'ao. "Medical Ethics in Ancient China." *Bulletin of the History of Medicine* 13 (1943): 268–77.

Legge, James. *The Chinese Classics.* Vols. 1–5. Hongkong: Hongkong University Press, 1960.

Lenk, Kurt, ed. *Ideologie, Ideologiekritik und Wissenssoziologie.* Neuwied and Berlin: Luchterhand Verlag, 1961.

Lévi-Strauss, Claude. *The Raw and the Cooked.* Translated by J. and D. Weightman. New York: Harper and Row, 1969.

Lewis, Oscar. *Life in a Mexican Village: Tepoztlán Restudied.* Urbana: University of Illinois Press, 1951.

Liu Ming-shu. "An Invasion by Nan Chao and the Destruction of the Nestorians at Chengtu." *Frontier Studies,* 1942/44 (Chengtu, 1945), pp. 29–34.

Mair, Lucy. *An Introduction to Social Anthropology.* New York and London: Oxford University Press, 1972.

Maloney, Clarence. *The Evil Eye.* New York: Columbia University Press, 1976.

Mannheim, Karl. *Ideologie und Utopie.* Bonn: Verlag von Friedrich Cohen, 1929.

132   *Bibliography*

Martin, Jack D. "New dilemma for doctors: HMO advertising, Prepaid plans' horn-blowing for 'complete health care' is prompting a hard new look at the ethics of patient solicitation." *Medical Economics*, 19 August 1974, pp. 67–71.

Michaud, Paul. "The Yellow Turbans." *Monumenta Serica* 17(1958): 47–127.

Nash, June. "The Logic of Behavior: Curing in a Maya Indian Town." *Human Organization* 26(1967): 132–140.

Needham, Joseph R. *Clerks and Craftsmen in China and the West.* Cambridge: Cambridge University Press, 1970.

Scheler, Max F. *Formalism in Ethics and Non-Formal Ethics of Values: A New Attempt toward the Foundation of an Ethical Personalism.* Translated by M.S. Frings and R.L. Funk. Evanston, Ill.: Northwestern University Press, 1973.

Schoeck, Helmut. *Der Neid und die Gesellschaft.* Freiburg i.Br.: Herder, 1966.

Sharma, Shiv. "Ayurvedic Medicine in Practice." *Nihon Ishigaku Zasshi* 19, no. 4 (1973): 444–47.

Sivin, Nathan. *Chinese Alchemy: Preliminary Studies.* Cambridge, Mass.: Harvard University Press, 1968.

Unschuld, Paul U. *Die Praxis des traditionellen chinesischen Heilsystems.* Wiesbaden: Franz Steiner Verlag, 1973.

————. *Pen-ts'ao: 2000 Jahre traditionelle pharmazeutische Literatur Chinas.* München: Heinz Moos Verlag, 1973.

————. "Professionalisierung im Bereich der Medizin: Entwurf zu einer historisch-anthropologischen Studie." *Saeculum* 25(1974): 251–76.

————. "Medico-cultural conflicts in Asian settings: An explanatory theory." *Social Science and Medicine* 3(1975): 303–12.

————. "Arzneimittelmissbrauch und heterodoxe Heiltätigkeit im China der Kaiserzeit: Ausgewählte Materialien zu Gesetzgebung und Rechtsprechung." *Sudhoffs Archiv* 61(1977): 356–89.

————. "China." In *Krankheit, Heilkunst, Heilung,* edited by H. Schipperges, E. Seidler, and P.U. Unschuld, pp. 193–227. Freiburg: Karl Alber Verlag, 1978.

————. "Das Ch'uan-ya und die Praxis chinesischer Landärzte im 18. Jahrhundert." *Sudhoffs Archiv* 62(1978): in press.

Unschuld, Ulrike: "Traditional Chinese Pharmacology: An Analysis of Its Development in the Thirteenth Century." *Isis* 68(1977): 224–48.

Welch, Holmes: *Taoism, the Parting of the Way.* Boston: Beacon Press, 1957.

White, Paul E. "Resources as Determinants of Organizational Behavior." *Administrative Science Quarterly*, September 1974, pp. 366–79.

Index

Abortion, 48–49
Acupuncture, 16, 29, 37
Analects (Lun-yü)
    (Confucius), 38–39, 40
Ayurvedic medicine,
    protection systems in, 13

Bakweri people (West Africa),
    6
Bridgman, R. G., 39
Buddhism, 25, 48
    and medical resources,
        19–21

Chang Chan, 29
Chang Chieh-pin (fl. A.D.
    1624), 81–84, 107
Chang Jen (eighteenth
    century), 99
Chang Kao (fl. A.D. 1210),
    44–53, 57

Chang Lu (A.D. 1627–1707),
    84, 85–94
    and differential treatment of
        rich and poor, 86, 92
Chang Ts'ung-cheng (A.D.
    1156–1228), 58
Chang Wei-jen, 41
Chang Yen-ming, 52–53, 63
Chao Hsüeh-min (ca. A.D.
    1730–1805), 113
Che-kung man-lu (Huang
    Ch'eng-hao), 84–85
Chen Ch'üan (A.D. 541–643),
    57
Chen Li-yen (ca. A.D. 600),
    57
Ch'en Shih-kung (fl. A.D.
    1605), 76–80
Ch'en Tsu-yen, 45
Ch'eng Huang, 50–51
Ch'i, Southern, medical
    resources in, 19

Chia-i ching (Huang-fu Mi), 37

Chiang Ch'ou (fl. A.D. 1207), 42, 43

Chiang Shih (fl. A.D. 1895), 108

Chiang Shun-ming, 47

Ch'ien-chin fang (Sun Szu-miao), 25–27, 29–33

Ch'ien-chin i-fang (Sun Szu-miao), 25, 33–34

Chin dynasty (A.D. 265–420), 96

Ch'in dynasty (221–206 B.C.)

Chin Meng-shih (ca. A.D. 1600), 81

Ch'i Po (legendary), 92, 97

Chi-yen liang-fang (Nien Hsi-yao), 95

Chou Chin, 46–47

Chou dynasty (1122?–256 B.C.), 7

Chou-li, 22

Ch'uan-ya (Chao Hsüeh-min), 113

Chu Chen-heng (A.D. 1281–1358). *See* Chu Yen-hsiu

Chu Feng-hsiang (ca. A.D. 1590?), 60–61

Chu Hsi (A.D. 1130–1200), 41, 60, 95
  classification of medicine by, 39
  Hsiao-hsüeh of, 2 ill.
  and neo-Confucianism, 38–40
  on *wu-i,* 39, 40

Chu Hui-ming (ca. A.D. 1590), 60–66, 101
  deplored secrecy, 61–62
  ethical formulations, 62–66
  traditions, 60–61

Chu Kung (fl. A.D. 1088), 41

Chun-i ("military physicians"), 19

Chu Tzu-yang. *See* Chu Hsi

Chu Yen-hsiu (Chu Chen-heng; A.D. 1281–1358), 57, 58

Chün-i ("military physicians"), 19

"Common physicians" (*yung-i*), 23, 58
  in Chiang Ch'ou's thought, 42, 43
  distinguished from *ming-i,* 68, 69–70
  Hsü Yen-tso's critique of, 113
  Wang K'en-t'ang's critique of, 67–68

Compassion (*tz'u*)
  in Confucian thought, 20, 98
  in K'ou Tsung-shih's thought, 37, 38
  in Sun Szu-miao's thought, 27

Confucius and Confucianism, ethical positions of, 7, 42–58, 61
  Analects of, 38–39, 40
  becomes comprehensive ideology, 16–17
  internal debate in, 21–23

Confucius (Continued)
  ju-i (Confucian medical
    scholars), 15, 23, 25,
    42, 43, 58, 59, 60, 68,
    71–72
  medical knowledge in,
    17–18
  as paradigm, 7
  professionalization and
    specialization criticized
    by, 17–18, 85–95
  and Sun Szu-miao's
    position, 35–38
  values of humaneness and
    compassion, 20, 53,
    98, 99
  variety of medical experts
    under, 18–19
"Court physicians" (*t'ai-i*),
    26n, 28

Demonic medicine, 26–27
Drugs. *See* Pharmacotherapy

Eberhard, Wolfram, 119–20
Education, medical, 20–21,
    22–23, 27, 40
"Enlightened physicians"
    (*ming-i*), 40, 58, 59, 60,
    68, 84
  distinguished from *yung-i*,
    68, 69–70
Ethics, medical, 11–12
  defined, 11
  formulated ethics, 11–12,
    13
  as paradigm, 114, 115
  in professionalization, 5

Ethics (Continued)
  as protective device,
    120–21
  and new values, 121

Fa Ch'eng, 48
"Family traditional
    physicians" (*shih-i*), 59
Fan Wen-cheng kung, (A.D.
    989–1052), 98, 99
Five Phases concept, 16, 26
Fu Chu-chiao, 47
Fukien, 67

Germany, medical solicitation
    in, 68n–69n
Great Britain, medical
    solicitation in, 68n–69n
"Great Physicians" (*ta-i*), 26,
    28, 29–33
Greece, protection system for
    doctors in, 12
Group consciousness, 27–28,
    76–80

Han dynasty (A.D. 25–220), 7,
    18
Hangchou, medical
    examinations in, 22
Han-lin academy, 35
Han Mao (fl. A.D. 1522),
    56–57
Han-shih i-t'ung (Han Mao),
    56–57
Hartwell, Robert, 17
Hippocrates, 13
Ho Ch'eng, 51–52
Ho Ch'i-pin, 108–9

Hospitals, creation of, 18–19
Hsiao-hsüeh (Chu Hsi), 2
Hsien Yüan (Yellow
   Emperor), 92, 97
Hsü Chih-ts'ang (A.D.
   581–618), 57
Hsü Ch'un-fu (fl. A.D. 1156),
   40–41, 59
Hsüeh Chi (fl. A.D. 1530), 81
Hsü i-shuo (Chang Kao), 57
Hsü Lou-t'ai, 47
Hsü Shu-wei, 44–45
Hsü Ta-ch'un (A.D.
   1693–1771), 80
Hsü Yen-tso (fl. A.D. 1895),
   108–13
   critique of *yung-i* by, 113
   on drug use, 110–12
Huai Yüan (fl. 1809), 100–105
   on moral principles and
      character, 102–4
   on principles of medicine,
      104–5
   and value of prognosis, 101
Huan, Prince, 28
Huang Ch'eng-hao (fl. A.D.
   1636), 84–85
Huang Ching-kuo, 45–46
Huang-fu Mi (A.D. 215–82),
   37
Huang-ti, 40. *See also* Hsien
   Yüan
Huang-ti nei-ching (Yellow
   Emperor's Inner Classic),
   16, 27, 100
Huang Yüan-yü (fl. A.D.
   1755), 96

Humaneness (*jen*)
   in Chu Hui-ming's thought,
      62
   in Confucian thought, 20,
      53, 98, 99
   in Huai Yüan's thought,
      104–5
   in K'ou Tsung-shih's
      thought, 37, 38
   in Lu Chih's thought, 35,
      36
   in Sun Szu-miao's thought,
      27

I-ching, 98
Ideologies, 5–10
   as paradigms, 7–10, 117
   "pool of ideologies"
      concept, 7
I-hsüeh hui-hai (Sun Te-jung),
   105–6
I-hsüeh ju-men (Li Ch'an),
   59–60
I-kung ("medical craftsmen"),
   19, 20n
India, *ayurvedic* medicine in,
   13
Interests, 5–10
   paradigms and, 7–10
   in struggle for medical
      resources, 115
I-shuo (Chang Kao), 42–53,
   57
"Itinerant physicians"
   (*ling-i*), 15
I-ts'ui ching-yen (Hsü
   Yen-tso), 108–13

Jen. See Compassion

Ju-i ("Confucian medical scholars"), 15, 23, 25, 42, 43, 58, 59, 60
 in Kung T'ing-hsieh's thought, 71–72
 and *ming-i,* 68

Ko Ch'ien-sun (fl. A.D. 1348), 53–55

K'ou Tsung-shih (fl. A.D. 1116), 37–38, 101n

Ko Ying-lei, 54

Ku-chin i-ch'e (Huai Yüan), 100–105

Ku-chin i-t'ung ta-ch'üan (Hsü Ch'un-fu), 40–41

Ku-chin t'u-shu chi-ch'eng (Kung Hsin), 68–70

Kula institution (Trobriand Islands), 6

Kung Hsin (A.D. 1600), 68–70

Kung T'ing-hsien (fl. A.D. 1615), 70–74, 76

Kuo-i ("state physicians"), 40

Ku T'ing-lin (Ku Yen-wu, A.D. 1613–82), 106–7

Kwakiutl Indians (British Columbia), potlach institution of, 6

Lai Fu-yang (fl. A.D. 1596?), 41

Lao-tzu (604– ? B.C), 18, 28, 32

Legalism, 7

Legge, James, 39

Lewis, Oscar, 5

Liang-i ("good physicians"), 40

Liang-p'eng hui-chi (Sun Wei), 95–96

Li Ch'an (fl. A.D. 1575–80), 59–60

Li Chung-tzu (d. A.D. 1655), 67

Li Han-chang (A.D. 1821–99), 106–8

Li Hung-chang (A.D. 1823–1901), 106

Li Kao (A.D. 1180-1251), 57, 58, 81

Lin Ch'i-lung (seventeenth century), 75–76

Ling Chih-t'iao (fl. A.D. 1738), 95–96

Ling-i ("itinerant physicians"), 15

Ling-shu, 98

Lou Ts'ai, 45

Lu Ch'i (A.D. 1614–?), 84–85

Lu Chih (A.D. 754–805), 35–37

Lu Yang, 48

Mai-ching (Wang Hsi), 53

Malpractice legislation, 23n

Mannheim, Karl, 8

Marxism, as paradigm, 7

"Medical craftsmen" (*i-kung*), 19, 20n

Medical practice, in ancient China, 15–24

Medical systems, 3–5
  defined, 3, 4
Medicine, protective systems
  for, 12–14, 120–21
Mencius, 36, 61
"Military physicians"
  (*chün-i*), 19
Ming dynasty (A.D.
  1368–1644), 85
Ming-i ("enlightened
  physicians"), 40, 58, 59,
  60, 72–73
  distinguished from *yung-i*,
  68, 69–70
Ming-i ("renowned
  physicians"), 84
Miu Hsi-yung (seventeenth
  century), 107
Mohism, 7
Moral value of healing,
  upgrading of, 95–106
Moxibustion, 57
Muslim physicians, 21n

Nan-ching, 53
Nan-yang huo-jen shu (Chu
  Kung), 41
Navaho Indians, 4
Needham, Joseph, 21, 39,
  118n
Nestorian oculists, 21n
Nieh Ts'ung-chih, 45–46
Nien Hsi-yao (fl. A.D. 1725),
  95

Pan Ku (A.D. ?–92), 37
Pao-chün, 50–51

Pao Mu-tan, 49
Paradigms
  comprehensive and partial,
    7–8, 11, 114
  ethics and, 11, 114
  ideologies and, 7–10
  and Mannheim concept of
    ideology, 8
  propagation of, 8–10
  valuation of, 10
Pei-chi ch'ien-chin yao-fang
  (Sun Szu-miao), 25
Pen-ts'ao, 98
Pen-ts'ao kang mu (Ming
  materia medica), 113
Pen-ts'ao kang mu shih-i
  (Chao Hsüeh-min), 113
Pen-ts'ao yen-i (K'ou
  Tsung-shih), 37–38
Pharmacies, establishment of,
  20n
Pharmacotherapy, 27, 73,
  95–96, 107
  Chang Lu on, 91–92
  in Ch'en Shih-kung's
    thought, 78, 79
  Hsü Yen-tso on, 110–12
  in K'ou Tsung-shih's
    thought, 37–38
  Sun Szu-miao on, 31–32
Physicians, categories of, 15,
  58–60, 68, 69–70, 118
  chün-i ("military
    physicians"), 19
  i-kung ("medical
    craftsmen"), 19, 20n
  ju-i (Confucian medical

Physicians, *ju-i* (Continued)
scholars), 15, 23, 25,
42, 43, 59, 60, 68,
71–72
kuo-i ("state physicians"),
40
liang-i ("good
physicians"), 40
ling-i ("itinerant
physicians"), 15
ming-i ("enlightened
physicians"), 40, 58,
59, 60, 68, 69–70, 72,
84
ming-i ("renowned
physicians"), 84
shih-i ("family traditional
physicians"), 59
ta-i ("Great Physicians"),
26n, 28, 29–33, 43, 68
t'ai-i (court physicians),
26n, 28
te-i ("virtuous
physicians"), 59
wu-i ("sorcerer-
physicians"), 39,
40–41
yung-i ("common
physicians"), 23, 42,
43, 67–71, 113
Pien Ch'io (legendary), 21,
65–66, 71, 86, 87, 92
Potlach institutions, 6
Professionalization, 3–5, 118
Confucian critique of,
21–24, 36, 85–95
defined, 4

Professionalization (Continued)
development of, 4–5
of "independently
practicing" physicians,
21–23
as protective system, 13
in Sun Szu-miao's thought,
54
Western and Chinese,
compared, 118–19
Prognosis, 86, 101
as protective system, 13

"Renowned physicians,"
(*ming-i*), 84
Resources, medical, 3–5, 20
allocation and distribution
of, 3–4, 6–7, 16, 43n,
118
Confucian ranking of,
97–98
and formulation of ethics,
12–14
Lu Chih on, 35–36
primary and secondary,
differentiated, 4, 16,
115–16
Righteousness, in Confucian
teaching, 53

Scheler, Max, 11, 13
Shen Ch'ien-lu, 108
Shen Chin-ao (fl. A.D. 1773),
106–8
Shen-shih Tsun-sheng shu
(Shen Chin-ao), 106–8
Shih-chi, 86

Shih-i (family traditional physicians), 59
Shih-yao shen-shu (Ko Ch'ien-sun), 53–55
Solicitation, in contemporary medicine, 68n–69n
"Sorcerer-physicians" (*wu-i*), 39, 40–41
"State physicians" (*kuo-i*), 40
Sun Szu-miao (A.D. 581?–682), 24–34, 43, 54, 60, 113
  categorization of physicians by, 28
  education and background, 25
  formulation of behavioral standards, 33–34
  on "Great Physicians," 26, 28, 29–33
  medical system of, 26–27
Sun Ta-lang, 47
Sun Te-jung (fl. A.D. 1820), 105–6
Sun Wei (fl. A.D. 1738–40), 95–96
Su Tung-p'o (A.D. 1036–1101), 75
Su-wen, 53, 98
Szu-ma Ch'ien (145–80? B.C.), 21–22, 87
Szu-sheng hsüan-shu (Huang Yüan-yü), 96

Ta-i ("Great Physicians"), 26n, 28, 29–33, 43, 68
T'ai-i ("court physicians"), 26n, 28

Tai Liang (A.D. 1317–83), 55–56
T'ang dynasty (A.D. 618–906), 22
Taoism, 7, 36
  in competition for medical resources, 18, 21
  and Sun Szu-miao's system, 25, 28, 32
Te-i ("virtuous physicians"), 59, 60
Tou-chen ch'uan-hsin lu (Chu Hui-ming), 60–66
Trobriand Islands, *kula* institution in, 6
Ts'ang-kung, 87
Ts'ang-kung Shun-yü I, 86
Tsang Mao-chung (ca. A.D. 1590), 60, 62
Tsun-sheng shu (Shen Ch'ien-lu), 108
Tuan Ch'eng-wu, 49–50
Tung Ch'en-fei, 102
Ts'u. See Compassion
Tz'ui Chung-hui, 49
Tzu Hsia, 39

United States
  "defensive medicine" in, 120n
  medical solicitation in, 68n–69n

Wai-k'o cheng-tsung (Ch'en Shih-kung), 80
Wan Ch'üan (fl. A.D. 1549–68), 99
Wang Chu-an, 46

Wang Hsi (A.D. 210–85), 53
Wang Huan (ca. A.D.
  1500–1550), 40
Wang K'en-t'ang (ca. A.D.
  1600), 67–68
Wang Yün (fl. A.D. 1821),
  105–6
Wan Mi-chai shu (Wan
  Ch'üan), 99
Wan-ping hui ch'un (Kung
  T'ing-hsien), 71–74, 76
Weber, Max, 17
Wei dynasty (A.D. 220–280),
  96
Welfare attitude, in Confucian
  China, 19–20
Wu-i ("sorcerer-physicians"),
  39, 40–41

Yellow Emperor (Hsien Yüan
  Huang-ti), 40, 92, 97

*Yellow Emperor's Inner
  Classic* (Huang-ti
  nei-ching), 16, 27, 100.
  See also *Ling-shu;
  Su-wen*
Yellow Turbans, revolt of, 18
Yin-yang concept, 16, 37, 98
Yüan dynasty (A.D.
  1234–1367), 20n, 22–23,
  55
Yüeh-jen (Pien Ch'io), 65
Yung-i ("common
  physicians"), 23, 58
  in Chiang Ch'ou's thought,
    42, 43
  distinguished from *ming-i*,
    68, 69–70
  Hsü Yen-tso's critique of,
    113
  Wang K'en-t'ang on, 67–68

Designer	Leigh McClellan
Composition	Viking Typographics
Lithography	Braun-Brumfield, Inc.
Binder	Braun-Brumfield, Inc.
Text	VIP Times Roman
Display	VIP Times Roman
Paper	50 lb. P&S Offset Vellum B32
Binding	Holliston Roxite B 53590